Dear Pitman Publishing Customer

IMPORTANT – Read Th

We are delighted to announce a special free ser
Simply complete this form and return it to the address o
A Free Customer Newsletter
B Free Information Service
C Exclusive Customer Offers – which have included fr
D Opportunity to take part in product development sessions
E The chance for you to write about your own business experience and become one of our respected authors

CW00322774

Fill this in now and return it to us (no stamp needed in the UK) to join our customer information service.

Name: Position:

Company/Organisation:

Address (including postcode):

Country:

Telephone: Fax:

Nature of business:

Title of book purchased:

Comments:

-------------------------------- **Fold Here Then Staple** --------------------------------

We would be very grateful if you could answer these questions to help us with market research.

1 Where/How did you hear of this book?
- [ ] in a bookshop
- [ ] in a magazine/newspaper
  (please state which):

- [ ] information through the post
- [ ] recommendation from a colleague
- [ ] other (please state which):

2 Which newspaper(s)/magazine(s) do you read regularly?:

3 When buying a business book which factors influence you most?
(Please rank in order)
- [ ] recommendation from a colleague
- [ ] price
- [ ] content
- [ ] recommendation in a bookshop
- [ ] author
- [ ] publisher
- [ ] title
- [ ] other(s):

4 Is this book a
- [ ] personal purchase?
- [ ] company purchase?

5 Would you be prepared to spend a few minutes talking to our customer services staff to help with product development? YES/NO

PITMAN PUBLISHING
The Business Publisher

Written for managers competing in today's tough business world, our books will help you get the edge on competitors by showing you how to:

- increase quality, efficiency and productivity throughout your organisation
- use both proven and innovative management techniques
- improve the management skills of you and your staff
- implement winning customer strategies

In short they provide concise, practical information that you can use every day to improve the success of your business.

FINANCIAL TIMES

PITMAN PUBLISHING

Free Information Service
Pitman Professional Publishing
FREEPOST
128 Long Acre
LONDON
WC2E 9BR, UK

MOVING AHEAD IN YOUR CAREER

MOVING AHEAD IN YOUR CAREER

Successful techniques for ambitious managers

WILLET WEEKS

PITMAN PUBLISHING

PITMAN PUBLISHING
128 Long Acre, London WC2E 9AN

A Division of Longman Group Limited

First published in Great Britain 1994

British Library Cataloguing in Publication Data
A CIP catalogue record for this book can be obtained from the British Library.

ISBN 0 273 60703 0

Typeset by Northern Phototypesetting Co. Ltd, Bolton
Printed and bound in Great Britain by Bell and Bain Ltd, Glasgow

The Publishers' policy is to use paper manufactured from sustainable forests.

10 9 8 7 6 5 4 3 2 1

Contents

Preface   viii
Introduction   ix

Part I THE WAY IN

 1 Setting your Goals   3
 2 Types of Meetings, Types of People   15
 3 Teeing up for the First Meeting   23
 4 Non-verbal Signals   29
 5 The Quilted Wall   37
 6 The Questioning Technique   47
 7 The Pro-active Negotiator   54
 8 Early 'Trap Questions'   61
 9 The Follow-through   68
10 Unorthodox Questions   75
11 Winding it up   81
12 The Second and Third Meetings   84
13 The Advice Visit   88
14 Putting it Together   97

Part II THE WAY UP

15 How to Measure your Political Skills   107
16 Upward Mobility   112
17 Lateral Relationships   133
18 Relations with Subordinates   159
19 When 'Good-bye' is the Best Answer   171
20 In Conclusion   186

Preface

Prophets of doom would have it that career progress is unlikely, even impossible, in a period of chronic unemployment. Worse, they see the loss of a job as a catastrophic, permanent career setback. I find this attitude even more alarming than the outlook for employment. Because it is so likely to be self-fulfilling, doomsaying presents a great – and unnecessary – threat to the morale of the individual with a problem to solve.

Realism does not have to tip over into pessimism, particularly if one is aware of certain overlooked aspects of the new job market.

True, we have to empty our minds of the old assumption that recessions are only a pause in the industrial world's inevitable march to prosperity.

True, we must recognise that career progress, whether modest or dramatic, is no longer the God-given destiny of every decent, hard-working, intelligent person.

What is readily available to such people is a particular kind of knowledge that has been sadly neglected by schools at all levels. It is also a competence that seemed extraneous when promotions and job openings came along as part of an ever-expanding economy.

SOME DANGEROUSLY NEGLECTED SKILLS

The neglected skills I am referring to are those of marketing one's own abilities. While professional progress in the years ahead is by no means an impossibility, it is most likely to be realised by those who use the most effective tools available to further their own legitimate self-interest.

The purpose of this book is to share this kind of know-how with anyone who perceives that trial-and-error in the management of career change is no longer an acceptable method for winning in the newly competitive world of work. Few people I see like to 'sell' themselves. However, the times ahead promise to make giving in to this widespread human reluctance an expensive luxury.

The techniques this book describes are those that have already served thousands of executives and managers well. However, they can only produce positive results if fuelled by a positive attitude. While it is important to recognise that we face a tough new job market, this is far from sounding a knell of doom. Here's why.

- Even an unemployment rate of 10 per cent means that 90 per cent of the job market is still actively functioning and is accessible to those with the right skills who address it in the right way.

- Not all of the reduction in situations vacant advertising is due to an absence of openings; often it is because organisations are increasingly using their voluminous files of spontaneous, direct applications to recruit candidates. Many directors of human resources ask themselves why they should spend money to advertise openings when they already possess a wealth of information on proactive people who, by writing, have demonstrated their initiative.

- Any director of human resources will testify that the great majority of applications they receive are so poorly presented as to guarantee an automatic rejection at first reading. This fact considerably thins the ranks of competitors.

- Finally, having the confidence that you are using the most effective methods of job seeking is in itself an immense builder of morale.

Reading about how to open doors to the future is only the beginning. Obviously the next and harder step is to put into action the advice you will find in these pages. As with any new skill, it is practice that makes perfect; there is, sadly, no magic formula for effecting a positive career change. There are, however, certain 'do's and don'ts' that can make the difference between success and failure. These I spell out.

Even after you have reached your immediate goal you will find yourself in possession of an invaluable new asset – a permanent assurance policy against the risk of professional checkmate.

Introduction

After 20 years of full-time activity as a career counsellor to people in management roles, I still feel sad and even resentful that many able executives are destined to accept jobs far below their real worth – and all for one clear, yet perfectly solvable reason: their inability to negotiate skilfully in their own interest.

Among over 6 000 people I and my colleagues have helped in their careers, I can recall a high proportion of executives whose behaviour in interview situations repeatedly blocked them from positions that I knew – and they knew – they were perfectly well qualified to fill. Often such people had already proved their abilities in the course of their careers – up to the point that they sought a change. In fact, many of them had previously enjoyed such progress and stability of employment that their seeming inability to negotiate suitable job offers came as a potentially dangerous psychological shock – dangerous because they viewed their failure to be selected in a highly damaging way, interpreting each turn-down as a rejection of themselves and the qualities they had to offer.

Many of us have seen the process unfolding at one time or another – perhaps in the case of a friend, a spouse, a business associate or even ourselves. First there is the optimism, then, with each 'rejection', an increasing erosion of confidence, followed by inner stress and a tendency to regard oneself a potential 'failure'. Successively we see the onset of bitterness and, finally, of a self-defeating despondency that can no longer be concealed from the interviewer. During the later stages of this process the self-image of failure can reinforce itself with each negative interview, with the risk of taking full control of whatever future contacts may be arranged.

My aim is to make available to you a precious quality that most of us lack. This quality is the ability to be objective about ourselves. The self-defeating process I have just described represents people's *subjective* views of themselves and their *perceived* failures. Day after day, my job is to help my clients step outside the confines of their situation, to see themselves as other people do and to apply, in their own individual way, certain basic principles of self-negotiation that have proved effective time and again.

I want to be clear that my aim in what follows is not in any way to present a manual on how to make contacts to find a job. There are already several books that describe various tested methods of arranging meetings with potential employers.

Basically, we are concerned here with what happens *after* you meet face to face either with a prospective employer or with a professional recruiter in the field of executive search.

We must accept at the outset that the employment interview is a very special type of human relationship. It is hard to imagine any other quite like it. One possible parallel, perhaps, is the moment when a person proposes marriage. Here the possibility of rejection certainly exists, but, for 'better or worse', sentiment is apt to have its way. Rarely, of course, is this the case in the world of business and the professions. Or perhaps we can cite the example of an interview for university admission. Here, too, there is a high risk of refusal but the element of negotiation is as notably absent as it is present in most senior employment interviews. Let us be clear, the job interview is a meeting that is unique in itself. Yet most of us enter into such exchanges carrying the same baggage of attitudes and habits that seem to have stood us in good stead in our other human relations, both business and personal. The trouble is that what works well in our usual transactions may not work at all in the competition for jobs and the professions.

So, we find ourselves face to face with the major cause of unsuccessful interviews: the failure to regard such meetings as different from others and to approach them as a unique kind of experience – demanding the learning of new attitudes and techniques. Horses, bikes and cars are all means of getting about, yet we are not likely to imagine that the same skills are required to control each of them. So why do many people believe that their abilities as salespeople, engineers or accountants will see them successfully through the negotiations that will lead to their ideal job?

No matter how many interviews you may have had in the past, stand back now and take a fresh look at what is really going on in such meetings. If you are willing to do this, you may well be making the best investment of your life. Just how do you place a monetary value on having a number of concrete options for the future? How can you measure the feeling of freedom that comes when you are fully confident that you know how to find a good job whenever circumstances tell you that it is time for a change? Though it may be hard to place a price on these elements of your career, there is obviously one factor that *can* be measured with some accuracy – your future salary. In this matter alone, the time and thought you give to your interview techniques will pay handsome dividends. For the more job offers you have, the stronger your negotiating position will be. And if your handling of each interview is skilful, you will be able to emerge with the best pay package possible in that particular situation. And, there is an additional bonus to be had from learning effective interview techniques: despite the fact that your business or professional experience may be of little help in 'selling yourself', the reverse is by no means true. Many of my clients – perhaps the majority – have found that their marketing and management techniques, as well as their ongoing human relationships, have benefited tangibly from their training in how to handle job interviews.

Now we have seen the very real value of a careful re-examination of your interview behaviour, but there is another step to be taken if such a study is to bring you the rewards it should. It is a simple requirement, but for most people it is considerably harder to achieve. It is to have a completely open mind on the subject. To profit fully from the successful experience of others you must be ready to discard a number of prejudices, illusions and practices that, like comfortable old shoes, we tend to carry on wearing simply because they give us no pain. Change is seldom achieved without discomfort.

Thus there are only two requirements if you are to profit from what follows: to accept that lifting the level of your negotiating skills is a matter of major importance to you and your family; and to be willing and ready to abandon many, perhaps cherished, ideas you may already have on the subject.

Unfortunately, among the case histories I cite there is an absence of career histories of women. The reason for this is clear; fewer than 10 per cent of my clients are female. Whereas from among hundreds of male clients I have been able to choose a number of histories to illustrate specific points, this has not been possible with women.

Why do so few women seek executive career counselling? The answer could be revealing. I suspect it has to do with discrimination since the percentage of my clients who are female probably roughly reflects the proportion of middle and upper managers to be found in business today. Happily, this situation is rapidly changing. Happily also, the histories I recount are as applicable to women as to men. I hope that the points they make will help many women redress the imbalance that exists.

As we take a fresh look at the ways to negotiate in our own self-interest, you should keep in mind the battery of expertise behind the person you will meet on the other side of the desk. Numerous books and articles in business magazines advise corporations on scientific executive selection, focusing often on the techniques of interviewing candidates. Corporate seminars are held on the subject. Professional psychologists and other specialists are often employed to back up the judgement of the interviewer.

And what similar expertise is at the disposal of the candidate? The answer is precious little, except perhaps for a few rather expensive executive counselling services of varying quality.

This book is intended to redress the balance in that I am aiming it at the individual. However, employers may also find some useful insights in these chapters. My own strong feeling may be novel but is, I think, valid: helping competent people to win their way to positions that give them real satisfaction and enable them to progress is a service both to the organisation and to the individual.

With this goal in mind, we will look now at the following question: 'What is really going on in the meeting known, misleadingly, as the "job interview"?'

Part I

THE WAY IN

Targeting and finding the right post

CHAPTER 1

Setting your goals

The indispensable first step in the process of optimisng your career is to fix your goals within the framework of reality. This process is very like a mechanical check-up of your car. What is its horsepower? Its braking capacity? Is it better adapted to the open road, city driving or rough terrain? What is its seating capacity and its fuel consumption? With this information in hand, you come to understand the possibilities and the limits of your car. A similar process is available to you in assessing your future career course and potential – as long as you are prepared to go back to the essence of your personality, character, and way of looking at your life and your work. This is not an easy exercise, but it can be an extremely rewarding one. Basically it consists of posing certain key questions to yourself, and answering them with all the honesty and objectivity you are capable of. We will start with four basic work choices.

1 To opt for increasing responsibilities in line management.
2 To continue to pursue your speciality in a non-management staff role whether this be, for example, laboratory technician, accountant, engineer, salesperson, etc.
3 To blend options 1 and 2 by seeking responsibility for an activity which in itself is basically 'staff'. Here we are referring to such posts as head of personnel, director of research, public relations director or chief economist. The departments in question do not directly turn the wheels of management; rather they provide certain resources that are invaluable to management. The key jobs are thus 'line within staff' since they carry line responsibility for a supporting activity.
4 To go it alone in your own business.

A useful way to discover the right answers for yourself is to match your own qualities and characteristics with those of the types of people who have proved successful in each of the roles listed above. What kinds of people are they? Which, among their qualities, are the attributes you yourself share? It should not be hard for you after this exercise to visualise in broad terms the future career path likely to be the most fruitful one for you in terms of job satisfaction and the possibility of growth.

THE TOP LINE MANAGER

This is a person who participates in the formulation of management decisions and is charged with carrying them out.

Your answers to the following questions should help you discern whether the road to top management is really the one for you or whether at some point in your progress you may find yourself at a dead end.

1. Are you really a good communicator?

The top manager almost always is. This does not mean that you habitually communicate what others are hoping to hear. Nor does it mean that you are necessarily a thundering orator. You simply have to have a way of getting across to others – whether on paper or face to face – the messages that you have in your mind and that you wish to transmit to others. Sometimes the messages may even seem obscure, but this is always your intention. In short, you must have control over the transmission of what is in your head and what you want others to understand.

2. Are you good with figures?

The top manager who is simply word-oriented – and many such people exist – is severely handicapped; being, to a greater or lesser degree, at the mercy of numerate people, who understand how figures can be manipulated.

3. Do you have the capacity to work long hours and long days – perhaps long weeks – when necessary?

The typical line manager has a high energy level, coupled with a motivation to see situations through to a resolution without counting the time or effort put in.

4. Do you habitually put your family at the top of your order of priorities?

I disclaim any responsibility for inventing the business world as it really exists. But the kind of person a top line manager probably is nearly always gives first priority to work. This preference is not inevitably as grim as it sounds, for such people often choose mates whose ambitions are comparable to their own and who are ready to co-operate in their advancement to what outsiders may sometimes regard as an unreasonable extent.

5. Are you basically optimistic in your approach to your work?

The term 'optimistic' is used here in a special sense. I call it 'functional optimism'. What I mean is that the top, or potentially top, executive sees problems in terms of their solution rather than in terms of the possibilities for disaster that they may pose.

The difference is illustrated to an exaggerated extent by the contrasting personalities of Chamberlain and Churchill.

6. Do you have the capacity, when needed, to manipulate the actions of other people?

Let's face it, those who are in power are usually good manipulators. They understand the motivations, the weaknesses, the fears and the strengths of superiors, associates and subordinates. However, they tend to be more preoccupied with the manipulation of the powers *above* them than with the personal concerns and needs of subordinates – though this lack of preoccupation downwards is frequently well concealed. In brief, top line managers do not permit sentimentality to rule their actions.

7. Do you have a streak of creativity or innovation?

The top line manager has a way of putting disparate ideas together to come up with new products and new paths for the future. This does not mean creativity in the artistic sense. It is more the creativity displayed by two young brothers in Akron, Ohio, USA, who from their bicycle shop had the thought that you might put together bicycle wheels, an internal combustion engine and wings, and end up with an apparatus that could fly through the air.

8. Are you hungry for information of all kinds?

Most top managers are. They devour information with a completely open spirit – for no reason perhaps except for their hunger to know. This zest for facts and opinions, and to soak up trends and new developments is closely linked to creativity. The continuous process of storing away disparate information provides managers with the raw material for combining seemingly unrelated ideas into something new and innovative.

9. Are you really prepared to put the well-being of your organisation above all considerations of sentiment?

If it is necessary to fire people to ensure the profitable continuation of the enterprise, the person in authority will do so with little hesitation, reasoning that the good of the entity takes precedence over the personal discomfort of any individual or group of individuals.

10. Do you prefer to avoid conflict?

The top line manager clearly does not. Indeed, they enjoy battles and look on life as a kind of test. Each time they emerge victorious in a clash, they feel strengthened in self-confidence. In a word, winning is a fundamental drive, whether it is a question of one-to-one combat or the overall triumph of the enterprise in the battle for markets and profits.

11. Do you possess intuitive intelligence?

Do you have the ability to make the right decisions quickly when there is little time for analysis and reflection? Effective managers will not always come up with the right choices at such moments, but it will happen often enough to ensure that the balance of results is on the positive side. Of course, they welcome situations that provide time for study; however, they are also ready to face up to emergencies and to take the decisions they feel are the best under the circumstances.

THE SPECIALIST

Specialists are perhaps less well paid but probably happier than the top line managers. They like, perhaps even love, their particular field of expertise. If they are tempted by early family ambitions or the values of others to move into important managerial functions, they risk looking back later on a major career blunder. And then it may be too late to switch into reverse. Does this person this sound like you?

1. Are you meticulous, caring profoundly whether each step is carried out as close to perfection as is humanly possible?

Specialists recoil from any shortfall from the ideal, whether they are involved in design, research, auditing or any other function which demands the utmost precision.

2. Do you have some hesitation in delegating work to others?

Because of your concern for work well done, do you frequently feel that you are the guardian of quality and thus tend to supervise the work of your subordinates very closely?

At times this tendency can cause resentment since, correctly or incorrectly, the others interpret this interference as a lack of confidence in their own abilities.

3. Do you tend inwardly to be sentimental in your relations with other true craftspeople?

When he shares with others similar ideals and aims, the human side of the specialist can be tapped. This only happens rarely, but when it does the specialist will defend the other person with little regard for any personal weaknesses or for their own real self-interest.

4. Are you a 'family-first' person?

We have already seen that many top managers have another order of priorities – in other words, business and career come ahead of family life in terms of their real interest. In contrast, the specialist speaks often of having a 'balanced life', of 'harmony' between career and personal activities. This probably means not only to spouse and children, but also hobbies – whether intellectual or otherwise.

5. Are you results-oriented?

Here specialists share a common quality with management. But there is a vast difference in the two definitions of the word 'results'. Specialists are probably referring to short-term results – the successful conclusion of whatever project is engrossing them at the moment. On the other hand top authorities must be thinking of longer term results concerning the position of the overall enterprise months and years into the future.

6. Do the words 'office politics' sound off-putting to you?

They do not to top line managers who see the game of acting in your own self-interest as a normal facet of business. The only emotional response to the subject is likely to be a determination to play the game more skilfully than everyone else.

7. Is earning a large salary high in your order of priorities?

This is, of course, a very subjective question. Everyone has their own definition of 'large'. However, the salary expectations of a top director are likely to be of quite a different order than that of the specialist. Then, too, in terms of priorities the line manager's chief motivation probably is not money but power. None the less remuneration is seen as recognition of success and thus it is a very important subject. Suffice it to say that excellent work performance is the driving force of the specialist with compensation usually taking a secondary role.

8. What kinds of reading do you prefer?

Do you tend to spurn general publications, preferring perhaps those dealing with professional matters? Do you shy away from fiction because it 'says nothing' to you? Perhaps you regard (and with some cogent arguments on your side) psychology and sociology as pseudo-sciences and thus without much interest? We have already pointed out the eclectic reading habits of most people in positions of command. Specialists are more 'practical', and have little zest for 'wasting their time' on extraneous reading or engaging in 'small talk'.

THE TEAM LEADER

Here we are speaking of the person who is best equipped to lead a team of people towards the realisation of a project or series of projects. This person is not a member of the top management of the organisation, and the job is probably a mixture of line and staff activities. Examples of team leaders are laboratory directors, product managers, general secretaries, chiefs of personnel and accountancy managers. The degree of responsibility can, of course, vary widely and the effectiveness with which the team leader can handle each level depends to a large degree on the mix of line manager's and specialist's qualities.

To help you sort out how closely your profile matches that of the team leader, let us examine some of the chief characteristics.

1. Do you empathise with subordinates?

Team managers display strong downward loyalties and tend to relate more readily to the team than to management. They mix with 'their' people and are concerned for their progress and the state of their morale. If they think that one of the team is being treated unjustly they will rise to that person's defence.

2. Do you have a tendency to make too many autonomous decisions?

One consequence of this 'downward orientation' can sometimes lead to neglect on the part of the team leaders to check out their decisions with management before taking action. As a result of this leaning towards autonomy team leaders can find themselves on the defensive, when later on it may become necessary to explain the reasons for their actions to their bosses.

3. Is the lack of clear general directives from management likely to be a major source of discontent?

Team leaders are not entrepreneurs; they are not very likely to be people who would relish the rigours of holding ultimate power within an enterprise. But at the same time there is a strong autonomous streak in their make-up. A good company for a team leader is a company whose direction and policies are clear, rational and, above all, are communicated through the various echelons of responsibility. Without this framework of guidance, the team leader feels ill at ease, with a sense of swimming in no particular direction, and this lack of security may show itself in a less and less concealed hostility towards the powers-that-be.

4. Do you sometimes place too much confidence in the people working for you?

We have already seen that top line managers are usually distinguished by a lack of sentimentality. Even specialists take pains to check up closely on the performance of the people who participate in their efforts. However, team leaders sometimes attribute to other people their own qualities of dedication, and preference for frank and open communication between team members. It is not rare for such a person to be both astonished and hurt when one of 'their people' fails to share in these ideals – perhaps even to the extent of engaging in manipulations over the team leader's head with management.

5. Are you by nature optimistic or pessimistic?

The team leader tends to be neither an optimist nor a pessimist. Many chief accountants, for example, lean towards functional pessimism for the simple reason that this is the safest course of action. On the other hand, a product manager must possess a positive personality in order to motivate the team to produce the best results. In either case we can generalise by saying that team leaders seldom, if ever, fall into a negative mood the severity of which is likely to interfere with the proper carrying out of their functions.

6. Do you give appropriate attention to detail?

If so, you are standing mid way in this respect between the top line manager and the specialist. Top line managers must force themselves to concentrate on some relatively small matters, knowing that the neglect of certain kinds of their 'homework' can result in troublesome consequences. On the other hand specialists relish details because they see them in terms of the overall excellence of the result they are trying to produce. The team leader in this regard, as in several others, has a more balanced view.

7. How good are you at selling yourself and your ideas?

Neither team leaders nor specialists are outstanding in impressing authorities or possible future employers with their strong qualities. Both prefer to let the results speak for themselves. Very likely both have been formed in an atmosphere where modesty was considered a prime virtue. Here we find another sharp point of departure with the top manager.

8. Are you results-oriented?

This consideration is closely linked with that of selling yourself. You expect that the results of your efforts will speak for themselves and will be recognised by management without the need for any self-promotion. Unfortunately, as often turns out to be the case, management's attention frequently is found to be concentrating on other matters. The resulting frustration is often described as a feeling of 'lack of justice'. In fact, the word 'justice' recurs frequently in my conversations with team leaders.

9. Do you have a quality of impulsiveness?

Here we arrive at a point of potential vulnerability in the case of many team leaders. With a certain inward confidence in their own qualities, but also squeezed between the precision of specialists and the distractions of management, they can easily become victim of an understandable frustration. At the same time they lack skills in office politics, as well as an outlet for their frustrations. The result can sometimes be a growing resentment at their lack of progress and rewards, culminating in actions that are not in their own self-interest. These can take the form of complaints to their colleagues about the quality of the management of their enterprise, through a kind of passive aggressiveness in group sessions, up to an 'I'm fed up' explosion in the front office.

THE ENTREPRENEUR

The characteristics of the real entrepreneur – someone who builds their own business – depart radically from the three profiles we have just examined. In fact, my experience shows that not more than 5 per cent of the executive population possesses the particular qualities required for success in their own enterprise. And even when the necessary psychological components are present, there still remain the practical considerations of having the necessary capital and finding the right product or service to market.

The real danger for many people is escapism – the desire to bolt from the 'system' – to satisfy a taste for freedom. This kind of motivation is all too understandable in the case of people who are in jobs that they find increasingly intolerable. Yet, before taking a decision, they owe it to themselves to make as objective an analysis as possible of their chances of success in 'going it alone'. To help in this endeavour, these are the main characteristics that I have identified as belonging to the most successful founders of their own enterprises.

1. Do you have a real need for recognition by others of the merit of your performance?

Entrepreneurs are generally confident in their own evaluation and recognition of the quality of their work. They have no superiors to provide this for them. At the same time they are aware of the dangers of relying for their self-esteem on the flattery of any subordinates they may have.

2. How tough are you?

If you are an entrepreneur, quite simply, you will do whatever is necessary to make your enterprise flourish. This can include weeding out, without mercy, unproductive people. It may well imply a certain exaggeration of your prospects in presentations to banks and other capital sources. You must be merciless towards the competition or any other possible threat to the health of your enterprise. Whatever sentimentality the entrepreneur possesses is reserved for activities outside of business life.

3. Just how high is your energy level?

If you mount your own business you can expect demands on you that other people cannot readily imagine. In periods of crisis or opportunity a 14-hour day, 7 days a week, is normal. At the start, you may be surprised, but must not be confounded, by the amount of detail you have to deal with without the specialised support you unconsciously relied on when working within an enterprise. You may have to arrange your own travel, be your own secretary and keep up with the figures, while at the same time filling the role of top salesperson.

4. Are you ready to neglect your spouse and children?

This may seem a brutal question, but the description above implies the possibility of just that. Nearly everyone possesses a conscience in this regard. If yours is too tender, you should seriously question the wisdom of launching out independently.

5. Ask yourself one simple question: 'What are the most important factors in getting ahead in business?'

There are two types of answers. The first type of reply centres on characteristics such as hard work, good human relations, integrity, production of ideas etc. These are not the replies given by the 'born entrepreneur', who is more likely to reply in the following vein: to have the right product, to have the right market, to be sure you are sufficiently capitalised. These are the automatic responses that can help you identify whether you really belong inside a company or whether you have the ability to go it alone.

6. How many of the qualities of the top line manager do you share?

It is evident that, despite the particular characteristics of entrepreneurs, they are also cast into the roles of top managers described earlier. It is in this respect that many creative founders of enterprises fall short. They have imagination and all of the qualities we are now describing. But, once the project is launched, their shortcomings in management are revealed. At this point, the installation of a more professional manager into the top role may be necessary.

7. Is material security high on your list of needs?

If this is the case, you are likely to experience heavy – perhaps intolerable – stress in the conduct of your own affairs. Cash shortages are almost bound to occur. There may be periods when, due to strikes or other situations outside your control, orders are just not coming in as needed. There is no need to prolong the list of contingencies that can arise; there are many of them. Suffice it to say that the role of entrepreneur is not one that should seriously tempt the security-minded person.

There is probably no individual who fits all of the descriptions listed above. However, it is entirely possible for you to position yourself in the category which most reflects your qualities. You will then be able to state to present or future members of management your own preferred path for future progression. Without this kind of self-examination you are almost bound to be handicapped in your negotiations. In other words, the question will always remain: just what are you negotiating *for*?

WHAT KIND OF BUSINESS?

Up to now we have been discussing the kinds of roles you might best be suited for. The question of what industry or what types of activity to choose is less difficult to answer. Many people – civil engineers or specialists in electronics, for example – have the question answered for them automatically because of their prior training. As for people with more transferable skills – including finance, sales and general management – it makes sense to gravitate towards the kinds of enterprises which, quite simply, interest them the most.

For example, I find among my clients certain people who have a marked leaning towards creative work. There is little reason for such a person not to direct their career towards publishing, advertising, or even television or the movies – if their skills really are widely adaptable to a variety of company settings. Obviously a salesperson who has been selling heavy industrial goods or technical equipment to industry will not fit readily into the fashion business or any other activity selling to the public. A finance person lacking experience of costing products will simply be dreaming if they contemplate entering a manufacturing enterprise where every step of the process is centred on the equation of cost versus return.

WHAT SIZE OF ENTERPRISE?

The size of the company that will suit you best may well depend upon your desire for autonomy and how skilled you are at office politics. The specialist and the team leader, for example, have strong elements of independence in their make-up. They will probably make full use of their zest for assuming responsibility for their performance, either in smaller organisations or in subsidiaries of large companies where the subsidiary is not too tightly controlled. Frequently the foreign subsidiaries of multinational companies could fit such a person well. On the other hand, the top line manager could do well to opt for a big operation. Here the potential ceiling is unlimited, as the top line manager prefers it to be, the element of competition for the top spots is always there and full play can be found developing manipulative skills.

I hope these hints will prove helpful to you in charting your future course of action. In any case, either with the help of outside advice, or by suitable reflection on your part, you are by now aware that the evolution of a rewarding executive career is not just a matter of accident; it is not the result of simply seizing the opportunities that happen to present themselves in the course of time, but rather of preparing yourself to fit such opportunities into your long-range development.

CHAPTER 2

Types of meetings, types of people

In the development of your career, you can expect to face two types of meetings that are very different in nature. They are:

- meetings with future employers; and
- meetings with executive search or recruiting organisations.

The person conducting the first type of meeting may have the power to make a final decision.

Conversely, any kind of independent recruiter is acting in the role of intermediary. Standing between you and the client company, the recruiter acts as a filter, permitting some candidates to meet with the final hiring authority, while barring the way to others. Because of their independent position outside the hierarchy of corporate power, the executive searcher's stance is one of objectivity; on the one hand, they have a set of job specifications (which they may have helped to put together); on the other hand, there is you, with your particular combination of experience, skills and personality. Determining the degree of overlap between these elements is the executive searcher's job. The work is entirely rational and you are not faced with the challenge of 'closing a sale'. The good recruiter is likely to be a highly professional interviewer who well knows the kind of information to look for and how to go about obtaining it. Attempts on your part to manipulate the meeting will do little more than waste time. Only well-marshalled facts, coupled with a compelling way of presenting them, will see you successfully through the searcher's screening to a face-to-face contact with the client.

MEETINGS WITH EXECUTIVE SEARCH FIRMS

Here are a few hints that will be useful in the handling of such meetings.

Executive search firms are not career counsellors

It is not the business of executive search firms to advise you on radical changes of career. As their fee is 20 to 30 per cent (or more) of your projected annual salary, they simply cannot take risks. Do not waste their time discussing how you would like to be an airline pilot if your experience reveals that you are a highly competent sales engineer. Forget imaginative solutions; for the executive searcher, the question is, does your job history project neatly and clearly into the situation at hand? In many cases, the interviewer will help you address yourself to this question by providing you with a clear statement of the requirements of the position.

However, you cannot count on this. Often you will have to put forward your own history first in order to allow the searcher to make an evaluation uncontaminated by your own views on the closeness of the fit. If this 'blind' approach is used, you can do very little, other than to interject questions whenever possible, hoping to collect fragments of information about what the interviewer has in mind. Your chances of success in this are, frankly, small. You can take encouragement from one positive fact, however. You would not be in the meeting at all if the recruiter did not have at least minimal information – probably from your résumé – about your background and qualifications. To this degree you start your meeting on a positive note.

Security

Always assume there is a very good reason behind the invitation you have received to meet with a search firm. This may sound obvious, but it is not. Such meetings are often proposed in a thoroughly disarming fashion. The letter or telephone contact may go along these lines: 'Please understand that the purpose of this meeting is simply to make your acquaintance – nothing more.' Or, 'While we have no particular post in mind, I would like to spend a few minutes with you to discuss your situation in more detail.'

Such messages may or may not be totally frank. They are probably not. One reason for this is the habitual reluctance of a search firm to reveal the name of its client. If the client company is unique in its field and highly visible, any description at all, even the most generalised, might compromise confidentiality. Or the searcher may be proceeding to screen candidates before actually signing a contract with the client company, being convinced that the signature is forthcoming and knowing it will look good if a selection of qualified candidates can be delivered promptly after the deal is closed. In this case, the searcher will be particularly sensitive on the matter of security. After all, the competition is adept at quickly picking up signals that might lead to sources of new business.

A third possibility, of course, is that the message disclaiming any specific motive may mean just what it says – that no concrete offer does, indeed, exist. However, the candidate is still well advised to assume that the opposite is the case. After all, a top executive search firm is likely to be a busy place, occupied either with fulfilling existing search contracts or with seeking new ones. Logic dictates that the time available to devote 'let's get acquainted' sessions is at a premium. To ensure that you are suitably on your mettle in such meetings, you should assume that every appointment is – directly or indirectly – about a specific job opening.

Use discretion in your questions

Remind yourself before each meeting that the person you are about to see is not a member of the management team of the company they are representing. Nor, except in the case of certain highly specialised executive search agencies, is the searcher a fount of sophisticated technical knowledge. The searcher's expertise is in human relations and it is a mistake to assume that a wealth of detailed information is available – either concerning the inner workings of the client company or the ins and outs of the day-to-day activity of the post in question.

This is not to suggest that you refrain from posing questions. Instead, you should stick to fairly broad matters – sales volume, number of employees, general management style etc. Questions of this sort serve to show your interest and help prevent the discussion from becoming entirely one-sided. But beware of insisting on too much technical detail. Your interviewer simply may not possess the facts. This can lead to embarrassment – and embarrassment on either side of the desk is unwelcome, as it can damage the atmosphere.

Arrange another meeting

Do not leave the meeting without making every effort to establish a date for further contact. This principle applies to any type of employment meeting, but it is particularly important in meetings with recruiters. Reputable search firms are diligent in the matter of reporting back the results of their screening. It is not always the case, however, that they are prompt in sending out news of a negative result. As a consequence, the candidates may falsely believe that several of their meetings are in the process of developing towards a happy conclusion. This information gap can be not only troublesome but also downright dangerous. Other opportunities may be awaiting a decision from you as to your intentions. If you are expecting one or more positive replies from other sources you may delay following through on live possibilities. In this case, delay can be fatal. You may find out too late that the answer is 'no' from the search firm, but that the other possibility had dried up because of your delay.

To make sure that you do not come up against this problem, the procedure is quite simple. Usually the recruiter will close the first meeting with some statement like: ' We will be in touch with you as soon as we sort matters out.' You might well respond: 'Can you tell me about how long that might be?' Be prepared, of course, for a fairly vague reply: 'Oh, I imagine around three or four weeks from now.' This is your opening. Take out your diary. Calculate the date four weeks ahead and suggest that you contact the recruiter on that date. The chances are that there will be no objections, but even if there are, memories are not long and you are still perfectly at liberty to check in with the recruiter around the day in question. You are always better off living in reality. If the result is negative, this is information you should have as promptly as possible. Otherwise you may be harbouring false hopes that might demotivate you in your energetic pursuit of other possibilities.

MEETINGS WITH COMPANIES

In general, then, only a minimum of manipulation is possible or even to be recommended in meetings with executive recruiters. As already pointed out, a meeting with a manager within the enterprise of the prospective employer is a transaction of a very different nature. You can expect to be meeting people who want to know exactly how your experience and personality can be adapted to the needs of the organisation of which they are an important part.

We will call them 'decision makers'. They know what the company needs. Perhaps the immediate needs have already been wrapped up in the form of a job specification – perhaps not – depending on when and how your contact was made. In either case, the manager across the desk from you has, first, a broader view than the recruiter on corporate operations and, secondly, far more freedom of action.

Most personnel managers will not disagree if I do not group them under the heading of 'decision makers'. True, they may have a yes or no voice on the hiring of certain types of people, but this is seldom the case with middle and upper level managers. In certain situations, you may find yourself passing through the hands of the personnel manager in the form of a 'preliminary screening interview'. This should not happen very often. Certainly any search that commences with an executive recruitment firm will probably be conducted without any reference whatsoever to the personnel department.

Confining ourselves, then, to decision-making executives, you will – broadly speaking – be dealing with people who show a bias towards one of three styles in their conduct of pre-employment meetings. These three styles are as follows:

1 the pressure meeting;
2 the 'comfortable' meeting;
3 the rambling meeting.

THE PRESSURE MEETING

The name says it. This technique – an effort to put the candidate on the defensive (and to see how they cope) – was developed into something of an art form in America in the 1980s. Few managers today indulge in out-and-out mental torture, but none the less there are still many tough executives and professional people who like to put the applicant under psychological pressure. Past career decisions will be questioned, the reasons why you are on the job market will be probed in detail and your accomplishments will be minimised.

The fatal error in handling such situations is that the candidate may feel that the interviewer is showing hostility. Here is one sure sign that emotion is threatening to control your conduct. To ensure a correct response, you must first understand the probable motivations of the other person. Is the interviewer really manifesting sadistic tendencies? This is unlikely, but if it is true your problem is simplified; this person is hardly going to be the boss you are looking for.

Probably the real explanation of an aggressive approach is quite a different one. The interviewer may well be seeking information that is not readily reduced to the form of an oral résumé. Primarily the interviewer wants to know what kind of psychological stuff you are made of. How do you handle pressure? How do you react to aggression? What is your threshold of anger? To see these 'attacks' in this light can be liberating. Your own responses and the manner in which they are stated can swiftly change the meeting from a kind of inquisition to a real exchange of information. Only two things are required of you:

1 keep your cool, helped by your understanding of what is really going on;
2 make full use of questions in order to slow down the pace of the interviewer's questions and, above all, to give yourself time to think.

I recall one client who was determined to quit the diplomatic service for a post in the business sector. Though his only commercial experience was second-hand, centred on his observation of conditions in many foreign countries, we together succeeded in arranging more than 15 interviews with decision makers. One of these was with a high-flying company in financial investments. The managing director opened the meeting with a bizarre and improper question: 'Are you a religious man, Mr Smith?' The only other question in that meeting was: 'Are you a rich man, Mr Smith?'

My client's diplomatic background proved its value here. He did not answer either question. Rather than fumbling for a direct response, he came back with more question: 'May I ask in just what sense you are using the word "religious"? Are we speaking in philosophical terms? Of a moral code? Or perhaps of day-to-day religious practice?' His handling of the second question was similar: 'There are many ways of being rich – financially, intellectually, emotionally. Tell me, which do you have in mind?'

The upshot of the meeting was a second meeting and ultimately a job offer. This experience illustrates how questions, skillfully handled, can transform a meeting with little apparent prospect of success into one with a positive outcome.

The 'comfortable' meeting

Here the scenario is entirely different. The interview is relaxed – and relaxing. Perhaps the interviewer is not installed behind a desk, but waves you genially towards two upholstered chairs facing a coffee table. The interview commences with easy small talk – but don't be fooled. There is no small talk in such meetings.

The interviewer is really seeking facts and knows that the more at ease you are, the less defensive, and the less defensive, the more forthcoming you will be. The overriding danger, in fact, is that you will be tempted to talk too much. Feeling that the meeting is safely launched on an adult to adult basis, you are seduced by the cordiality of the interviewer into letting down your guard. Among the many examples of what can happen in such situations, one in particular stands out. A client of mine was well into a meeting with a managing director of an electrical manufacturing company when the latter asked the name of the candidate's boss. The name was forthcoming and the conversation switched to another subject. However, later the host 'wondered aloud' why my client wanted to quit an obviously fine post as technical manager. The candidate made some rather meaningless noises about 'incompatibility', but then was asked about the reasons for this incompatibility. As he said later, his response 'just seemed to slip out'; he stated there was a problem with alcohol that affected his superior's judgement and his relations with his executive team. To finish matters off the applicant expressed his concern about the direction in which his company seemed to be heading. The meeting went on for 20 minutes more. But there was no talk of a second meeting – only a vague promise to 'get back in touch'.

Back in my office, my client groaned: 'It was only at lunch after the meeting that it dawned on me what I had done. Not only was I saying things that were damaging to my company, but I'd also left behind the name of a poor guy having a bout with the bottle.'

'I wish I hadn't said that' is a phrase I've heard on many occasions and usually after a 'comfortable' meeting.

By now you will not be surprised to read my formula for coping with this particular type of danger. It is the same one as before; namely, to ask questions. If the other person is really as open as they seem, they will reply in an informative way, giving you facts that you should have if you are to understand, and relate to, the situation and needs of the company. More important, of course, is that fact that you cannot possibly be carrying on a monologue at the same time that you are motivating the other person to do most of the talking.

The rambling meeting

Not all executives and professional people are dedicated interviewers. One reason may be that their need to perform this task is only sporadic. Another reason is that they may resent the time required to screen a number of candidates, even while acknowledging intellectually the importance of such meetings.

There are two common ways that some pre-employment meetings seem to be wandering and disjointed, without any apparent sense of direction. One is the result of repeated interruptions due to the coming and going of assistants and colleagues, or to the ringing of the telephone. Another is marked by long silences, either because the interviewer's mind is elsewhere or because it is a part of their particular technique of dealing with people to lure them into a conversational vacuum.

If the problem is one of too-frequent outside interruptions in your exchanges, you have only one responsibility – that is to keep in mind what was being said at the moment the interruption occurred. The other person may be skilled at keeping track of several situations at once. Even then, there are likely to be some occasions when the interviewer's memory fails to click. At such times, the interviewer may murmur: 'Let's see, where were we?' You at least score a point for alertness if you are able to put the conversation back on its track.

As to how you handle periods of silence, this is for some people one of the most troublesome aspects of interviews. To try to 'out-silence' the other person not only makes for awkwardness, but can also develop a kind of test of wills. On the other hand, you certainly should not break in with some scrap of personal or professional history that is probably totally irrelevant or uninteresting.

Once again, we come back to the solution that has already been a demonstrated life-saver on other occasions. Ask a question.

CHAPTER 3

Teeing up for the first meeting

Because most executives and professional people make it a habit to plan ahead, they automatically ask themselves what steps they might take in preparing for a first encounter with a prospective employer.

Many people think that detailed research into the potential employer's company is the most useful kind of preparation. More often than not, they are surprised when I do not agree. Here is an example of what I mean. Among my clients was a sales and marketing manager with an excellent record of success in the men's clothing industry. Invited to a meeting with one of the world's largest textile companies, a British company, he set about learning all he could about the company. He studied the annual report in detail, obtained an analysis of future earnings prospects from his stockbroker and put a lot of questions to friends within the industry. Armed with a wealth of detail about the company, he arrived at the corporate headquarters confident of his chances – and with reason, since his experience matched up well with the profile of the product manager's job that was available.

In the event, he did not get the job. Worse, he was not even called back for a second meeting.

Both he and I were perplexed by his poor showing. Since this was one of the rare occasions when he and I were unable to pinpoint any probable sources of difficulty, I decided to telephone the vice-president who conducted the meeting to put the question to him. To my surprise he was surprised at my interest.

'You mean, he really wanted the job?' he asked.

'Very much,' I assured him.

'I'm really astonished. Frankly, he didn't seem very enthusiastic. He hardly asked any questions about the company and how it operates. This to me is usually a sign of a lack of interest, so at the end of our meeting I asked him outright if he had any questions. His reply was no; he felt he had enough information.'

Mystery resolved. Not for the first or the last time, I was reminded that too much preparation can be a dangerous thing. Your curiosity is inevitably dampened by a surfeit of information and this feeling that you 'know it all' in turn discourages the interviewer from carrying on with what may well be a favourite topic – the organisation the interviewer is a part of.

Common sense dictates, of course, that you should go into first meetings with some basic facts about a company's situation – total revenues, product line, number of employees, for example. Beyond this, however, the general rule should be that your best and most up-to-date source of information is very likely to be the person in front of you.

There is also another kind of preparation that can prove dangerous in certain situations. Do not take your CV into an employment meeting; it probably has been sent in advance in any case. Not only does presenting this piece of paper immediately pose a block to direct communication; it represents another possible danger as well. The interviewer may give way to a common human tendency to focus on possible points of weakness in the CV – a gap in dates, the sometimes sensitive matter of age, an MBA from a less well-known college. The danger of finding yourself on the defensive is all too apparent.

THE PORTFOLIO

On the other hand, there is another form of presentation that can, under certain circumstances, help you to highlight your successes dramatically. This is the creation of some form of scrapbook or portfolio. For an architect or advertising copywriter, this type of visual presentation is virtually a requirement. However, people in some other roles often overlook the fact that such a documentation could also be useful to them. Just how and if such a presentation can best be employed in meetings is a critical point. But first we should consider its possible contents.

The most effective portfolios work well because they display items of intrinsic human interest. Of course, charts and graphs showing how you improved sales and profit are among the possible displays, as are tabulations of cost-effectiveness and how you increased market share. These the other person may find of varying interest depending on their own background. But what everyone can understand and relate to are such human documents as newspaper clippings, citations, diplomas and, most particularly, photographs. Typical shots you might include are those taken at the time of a conference, an occasion when you received a award or even a picture of yourself engaged in an off-the-job hobby.

One client included in his scrapbook photographs of a greenhouse dedicated exclusively to his hobby of creating new species of hybrid azaleas. The success of one of his meetings – the one that led to his present job – can be traced to that sequence of pictures. Until the interviewer came across the three photos in question his attitude was aloof, almost negative. At that point, he thawed, stating that he also had a small greenhouse. The meeting in effect began anew, this time on a basis of understanding and a shared interest.

More common hobbies offer a wider chance to catch the attention of another person. Sailing, golf and tennis all offer the possibility of dramatic photos, and at the same time may strike a common chord with many interviewers.

How to use a portfolio

If you create a scrapbook or portfolio of any sort, you should avoid thrusting it under the nose of the other person. There are three reasons why this can be a serious mistake:

1 like the CV, your scrapbook is a potential obstacle to direct communication if it is offered at the wrong time;
2 the interviewer may interpret this as a confession of a need on your part for a kind of crutch to avoid the challenge of a face-to-face exchange;
3 you can lose valuable time as the interviewer randomly examines various pages. Indeed, you might find yourself out of time before you get around to discussing essential points.

You certainly should not place the scrapbook on the interviewer's desk (see Chapter 4). Keep it at your feet, preferably out of range of your interviewer's vision. The moment to present the volume is when the discussion touches on some point referred to in your documentation. Even then your use of the book should be dependent on a signal of interest from the other person. For example, a typical exchange might be as follows.

Interviewer: 'I'd like to hear more about your latest product launch for Hypo manufacturing. Exactly what were the results in terms of sales and profits?'

You: 'I have the figures in tabular form if you would care to see them.'

Your interviewer will almost certainly respond with a 'yes' and this is the opportune moment to display your portfolio. In other words, it should always be done at the interviewer's request rather than your own initiative. From this point on you are aided by the fact that curiosity is a trait which is common to most human beings. The interviewer is likely to spend a few moments with the figures and then to begin leafing through the other pages.

This manner of using the portfolio implies, of course, that you will leave some meetings with the book unopened. None the less, opportunities to present it will often occur. At such times a well-prepared scrapbook can score points for you, humanising the proceedings, highlighting your successes, and possibly establishing important common ground between you and a prospective employer.

WHAT TIME IS THE RIGHT TIME?

One aspect of your preparation for meetings is the matter of arriving at the 'proper' time. Having read this far, you should now be aware of the need to question conventional ways of thinking. You can be sure that the great majority of your competitors for posts are determined to behave in a 'correct' – or, to use another word, stereotyped – fashion. By behaving like this, they risk becoming blurred images in a grey sea of indistinguishable, executive job hunters. They do not pause to consider that the interviewer is probably in that position because of more dynamic qualities than an ability to think and act conventionally.

It is a good idea to question whether it is productive to arrive, as many candidates do, for a meeting in advance of the time scheduled. Almost always the receptionist is going to communicate your presence as soon as you announce your name. If your host is running a bit behind schedule – and this is not unusual in the routine of a busy executive – they may well be unable to receive you promptly at the agreed time. For example, a 10 minute delay on the interviewer's part would not be unusual. However, if you have arrived 10 minutes early, this means that you will have been sitting in the reception room for 20 minutes. This is enough time for many people to begin to get edgy. A factor which is equally important, however, is the knowledge on the part of your interviewer that you have been kept waiting for nearly half an hour. As a result the interviewer may hurry to finish the business in hand at the time of your arrival and will be left without a moment of decompression before you are ushered in.

I know of one situation where an early arrival was partly responsible for an appointment at an executive search firm that ended in total frustration. In this case, the receptionist did not ring through to the boss right away, since the applicant was 15 minutes ahead of the schedule. She ushered the visitor into a small reception room and said she would be back when the interviewer was free. Three-quarters of an hour later she returned carrying some magazines for the coffee table. The surprise on her face told the story. Time had gone by and she had forgotten to announce the applicant's arrival. Naturally, both receptionist and boss were very apologetic, but the damage was done. Most of the time set aside for the meeting had leaked away, and what remained was quickly filled in a sketchy and unsatisfactory manner.

So, arriving in advance of the agreed time is not always the best course of action. 'OK, point taken,' you might say, 'So the obvious right thing to do is to arrive exactly on time.' But is it really? Already on several occasions we have established that the right thing is not always the obvious thing and vice versa. Even punctuality should not be exempt from a healthy dose of scepticism. In the first place, it is a fair assumption that the person who is prompt to the second has probably spent some minutes loitering outside the premises in order to arrive with such precision. This could be seen as an over-concern with the small manifestations of 'good form'. If being on time is really a part of your nature and your way of doing things, you probably should follow your natural habit patterns in preference to arriving early. On the other hand, a third way exists of looking at the matter of timing your arrival.

There is, in fact, much to be said in favour of the course of action that I usually recommend to my clients; namely, that they show up just a few minutes after the agreed time. Most executives are grateful for whatever extra moments may be found during a busy day. For you to arrive five minutes late may well give your host a welcome chance to clear their desk or visit the lavatory (the lack of time for this activity being an endemic threat to executive nervous systems as well as good health). Furthermore, if you are careful to limit your lateness to around five minutes you do not run any risk of damaging the start of your meeting.

None the less, it is highly important that you do not, by misjudging the time needed to reach your destination, arrive too late. By aiming to be a little bit late your risk of being damagingly late by accident is, of course, increased. You must, therefore, be certain that you do not exceed the acceptable short period of grace. For this reason, I recommend to my clients that they make a dry run to the premises to be visited. Ideally, this should be done 24 hours before the time of the meeting so that traffic conditions are comparable. Such a scouting expedition permits you to clock exactly how long the journey will take. If you are travelling by car, you will want to check out the parking facilities in the area, if by public transportation, the location of the nearest train or bus stop.

The time and trouble involved in this kind of preparation can be well worth while. Few mistakes can be more demoralising than to misjudge your arrival time. The assurance that this will not happen to you permits you to start your meeting with maximum peace of mind.

CHAPTER 4

Non-verbal signals

At first I found the idea preposterous, but I am now convinced that at least 50 per cent of what we communicate to others is done without words. In fact, our very preoccupation with finding the right words may lead to us paying too little attention to the messages we are passing by other means – by facial expression, by the way we hold our bodies, by the gesture of our hands or by the way we dress.

To illustrate the point, I can best refer to a former American client with a multinational conglomerate who took part in an advanced executive training seminar in London. The group was made up of only 12 people, the atmosphere was informal and the group leader was an independent consultant with no knowledge of the background of the participants. He first introduced himself, then looked around the room and said: 'Ah, I see we have an American with us today. Welcome.' This was all very genial, but my client was puzzled. He had bought his suit in London in the course of an earlier visit, his family origins were Anglo-Saxon and he had not opened his mouth to speak. How, then, had the consultant identified his nationality so quickly? After the meeting, he put the question to him.

'The answer is very simple,' was the reply. 'I knew it from the way you cross your legs.'

He then explained that American males tend to cross the upper part of one leg with the lower part of the other, while Europeans affect a scissor-like cross with one knee-joint atop the other. He added that during the Second World War certain US agents had given themselves away in this fashion, despite covers that in every other way were impeccable.

In a similar way, it is amazing how often other people seem to know of thoughts and emotions at times when we are convinced we are not showing anything. At home, our children know when we are beginning to get angry almost before we ourselves are aware of it. A wife senses that there has been a problem at the office despite her husband's jaunty efforts at concealment.

The same kind of 'leakage' also occurs between people who do not know each other well. In pre-employment meetings we can benefit from non-verbal communications if we are aware of the signals we are emitting. However, seeing ourselves through the eyes of others is a notoriously difficult exercise. To help you do so, read the following list of some of the most common ways people reveal themselves non-verbally. I suggest that you pause as you note each mannerism to ask yourself if it bears any resemblance to your own habits. If you are in doubt, check with a colleague or your spouse for confirmation.

REVEALING NON-VERBAL SIGNALS

The invader

Writers such as Konrad Lorenz or Robert Ardry, who trace the evidence of primitive and animal behaviour in modern humanity, speak often of our unconscious drive to protect our 'territory', be it a cave, a plot of turf or – in the immediate case at hand – the space we occupy at work. Failure to respect the other person's territory can, and sometimes with reason, be seen as a signal of aggression. The job candidate who plumps a briefcase or any other article on the desk of the interviewer risks sending out a signal of invasion. In a less overt fashion, so does the person who rests their arms on the other person's desk. Don't do it!

Briefcases are best placed on the floor, conveniently to hand (not in your lap or you will look as uncomfortable as you probably actually are, with your arm motion hampered and your general demeanour that of readiness for instant flight).

The back-pedaller

The back-pedaller is the reverse of the invader. Some people unconsciously push back their chair a foot or two immediately on sitting down. Then, in the course of the meeting they tilt backwards, projecting a desire to put as much space as possible between themselves and the other person. Unless, for some reason, the chair was truly physically 'too close for comfort' the interviewer will subjectively size up such a gesture as that of a person who recoils from direct contact with others. The safe course of action, nearly always, is to leave the arrangement of the furniture to your host and, quite simply, to remind yourself to lean forwards (a motion that is expressive of your interest in what is being said) from time to time in the course of your meeting.

The window-gazer

An executive search firm I know occupies impressive offices on the thirty-sixth floor of a modern San Francisco office building. The magnificent panorama across San Francisco Bay was a deciding factor in the choice of these quarters. Imagine the dismay, then, that they felt almost as soon as the first visitors began to arrive. Potential clients, it turned out, showed themselves to be far more interested in the view than in the person facing them or in the message they were trying to get across. As a result, curtains now shroud the splendid – and no doubt very expensive – view.

In a less dramatic way, a job applicant can communicate – perhaps unjustifiably – a lack of interest by failing to look the interviewer directly in the face. I remember an exaggerated example of this shortcoming in the person of a top level civil servant who was seeking to make a move into private industry. Because of his proven ability he had been invited 25 times for meetings with companies. They were all his first – and unfortunately his last – meetings since he was never once called back for further discussions. Puzzled and frustrated, he came to me for advice.

His problem was very easily solved. Never in his life had this man been required to 'sell himself' on any other basis than his readily observable performance in his job. As he mounted the ladder of civil service grades through the years, he developed his own special mannerism in his conduct of meetings. He would swing his chair away from his desk, stretch out his legs and seem to address his attention – no doubt impressively and rather professorially – to his office window. Since he usually outranked the others at the meeting, he had no problem holding their attention. The same mannerism was, however, a disaster in his job search. He was surprised and a bit hurt when I told him that he was coming across as both arrogant (which was not really the case) and without any interest in the other person (nor was this true). Once he was able to see himself through the eyes of others, the problem was solved as easily as flipping a switch. He began to make contact in succeeding meetings and now, as a result, he is managing the affairs of an important industrial park.

Another person who comes to mind demonstrates the problem of many people whose progress has depended almost entirely on their technical skills. This was a shy computer technician who was very much aware of his difficulty in establishing warm human contact. Unfortunately, what he did not realise was that he had a real inability to look other people in the eye. He, too, was having difficulty in his pre-employment meetings. While his problem was also one of eye-contact, in this case I found the solution far from easy. In meeting after meeting he had to be reminded where to direct his gaze. Only after scores of such reminders and weeks of practice did his eye-contact begin to reach an acceptable level.

Here I must insert a caveat. There are some people who actually overdo the eye-contact, apparently because of a belief that they risk losing control of the situation by disengaging their gaze. The real risk lies in the other direction. By always focusing on the eyes of the other person, they can easily set off a kind of staring contest which is not only highly uncomfortable, but which looks like a contest for control.

Returning to the subject of primitive behaviour, we find even today that members of certain tribes interpret a direct stare as a signal of aggression. Perhaps a remnant of this attitude remains within many of us. If your meeting is with a person who is used to handling responsibility (it usually will be), you can also assume that they are accustomed to being in a controlling position a large part of the time. For this reason, I suggest that it is good practice for you to break direct eye-contact often enough to avoid any suggestion of a staring competition. This is not to propose that you become a kind of 'window-gazer', but rather that you simply shift your gaze fractionally, perhaps just over the other person's shoulder or toward the top of their forehead. Only such a minor refocusing is needed to avoid giving possible signals of over-intensity.

As to how you measure your own habits in the matter of eye-contact, you will probably have to rely on feedback from a friendly colleague. Pay attention to their views. Objectivity in this matter is difficult, if not impossible, to achieve without outside help.

The nervous chuckler

Is laughter a verbal or non-verbal means of communication? I include the subject in this section by simply labelling certain types of laughter or chuckling as a kind of tic. I am continually struck by the number of executives who produce a cross between a chuckle and a laugh at moments when there is nothing at all funny going on. No doubt the subconscious impulse is to prove that they are entirely at ease (even in a situation where the very serious subject of their future working life is up for discussion). The effect, of course, is the opposite. After the first few chuckles, the interviewer begins to feel uneasy. 'Is this person a lightweight?' the interviewer wonders, 'Or (horrors) is there something about *me* that is amusing?' Neither question, once posed, bodes well for the outcome of the contact.

I use the word tic because such laughter is usually a nervous habit. It is to be classified with certain verbal tics, such as the deplorable but common tendency to scatter the words 'you know' throughout a conversation. These things are not done consciously, but breaking the habit is not easy. In such situations, spouses or friends are of little help. The element of tension that produces the tic is simply not present in such everyday transactions. The only solution is to check yourself out by listening to yourself in the course of employment meetings. Are you certain you are laughing only at the appropriate times? Some interviewing executives are very supple in passing rapidly from light to serious remarks. Are you sure that you are altering your real mood at the same time? If you even suspect that little laughs are creeping into your exchanges at inappropriate times, your safest bet is not to laugh at all. After all, the meeting is a serious occasion. A smile will do.

The note-taker

I once knew a journalist whose speciality was interviewing famous people, particularly authors. Most of the people he talked to had immense vocabularies and the ability to turn an original phrase. Despite the nature of his subjects, my friend never carried with him a recorder or even a pencil and a paper. He was gifted with total recall and his articles were considered models of good reporting. Few of us, unfortunately, have this gift and as a result we find a certain number of compulsive notetakers in executive circles. Useful as the practice may be in other situations, there are several reasons for leaving your notebook at home when you set out for a meeting with a prospective employer.

- Your communication with the other person is bound to be disturbed to some extent at those moments when you are scribbling notes rather than focusing, as you should, your attention on the interviewer.
- The other person is likely to become a bit wary and less forthcoming with information about the company if everything that is said is being recorded on paper.
- There is inevitably the physical problem of where to place your notepad. If you put it on the interviewer's desk, you have then become an 'invader'. In your lap is an awkward procedure at best, even less graceful than using your briefcase as a table.

'But,' you may object, 'none of the above is a problem because I always ask first if the interviewer has any objection to my taking a few notes.'

But this is not, in practice, a solution since the interviewer will nearly always agree, if only to show that they are not going to be put off by such a detail. At the same time, however, they may wonder about your capacity to retain information.

It is better to write yourself an *aide-mémoire* right after the meeting. In this way you can avoid mixing up the content of various interviews – easy to do if you have succeeded in arranging several meetngs. A brief note like this can prove to be a boon when preparing for a second meeting with the same organisation.

The clammy clasp

To shake a moist hand is not merely disagreeable but also communicates a certain tension. Certainly some apprehension at the start of an interview is not unusual. If exaggerated, it may be due to your present situation (such as repeated rejections following meetings) or for causes that are basically psychological, such as shyness. The only practical advice I can give is that you should leave your right hand in your pocket until just before the greeting. Certainly, few gestures are less attractive than an attempt to wipe your hand surreptitiously on the side of your jacket.

BODY LANGUAGE

For those who can interpret non-verbal signals, the movements of the body constitute a rich field of observation. For example, some people remain as immobile as statues throughout an entire meeting, possibly thinking that they are projecting a message of self-control and imperturbability. If we accept that outer equilibrium is inner mastery imposed by self-control they may be right. None the less, talking with a statue is likely to be something less than stimulating. Then, too, there can be more than one reason for immobility. For instance, there is the person who is most unlikely to read a book like this. Here I am referring to the limp individual who is so undermotivated that they are simply lacking in energy and emotional tone.

With regard to posture, guard against either constant motion – a sure way to create a nervous atmosphere – and rigidity which is no more conducive than agitation to a good exchange. Listen to your body. If your position grows uncomfortable, then change it. Do not stay perched on the edge of your chair but sit back comfortably. When your interviewer touches on points that are important or compelling, do not hesitate to lean forwards at that moment. In so doing, you signal your interest in what the other person is saying through a movement that reflects attention to their words.

The language of hands may seem to be a detail, but it is a significant one. For the purposes of this book, the principal danger to avoid is the use of hand gestures that are too eloquent. Some people, without realising it, transform their fingers into symbolic daggers which they thrust repeatedly towards the interviewer. The interviewee may simply be eager to reinforce the points they are making, but instead these gestures can be interpreted as signs of aggression. If you have this habit, train yourself to rest your hands mostly on your knees.

Paul's method

Among the several clinical psychologists with whom I have worked, one in particular inspires the confidence and respect of his clients. Others might surpass him in physical or even intellectual stature; yet Paul invariably radiates an impression of solidity, regardless of circumstances. A flourishing beard, granny glasses and sober garb help create this impression. Above all, however, he displays a remarkable self-possession when confronted with delicate questions to which he is not sure quite how to respond. Everyone from time to time finds themselves in such a situation.

I have often observed Paul at moments like these. He sits far back in his chair and crosses his hands (never his arms which suggests a defensive attitude), then he tilts back his head and fixes his gaze on a point about 45 degrees above the horizon. After some moments of silence he drops his gaze to look the other person directly in the eyes, then delivers his reply calmly.

'You make me think of Moses receiving his message from on high,' I said one day.

'Good,' he said. 'Now let's try the usual method.'

With that he imitated the attitude of many people when seeking the answer to a tough question: head lowered, regard fixed on nervously twisting hands, projecting the image of a person grappling with a heavy, probably unsolvable, problem.

The contrast between the two attitudes was striking. On the one hand we see a person comfortably sure of an imminent resolution of the problem, thanks perhaps to some heavenly intervention. On the other we see an anguished individual, trapped and teetering on the edge of defeat.

Try out each of these roles with a friend. I am sure you will find Paul's method effective.

The Bearded One

In contrast to certain professional people like Paul, not many businessmen wear beards. Those who do so in a corporate setting tend to be scientific researchers or creative people, perhaps in advertising. When one of my clients prefers to sport a beard, I resist the temptation to try to dissuade him. I feel obliged, however, to remark that his preference is likely to be a handicap in his search for career advancement. One convincing argument I sometimes employ is to ask the person to visualise the beardless faces of popularly elected leaders of Western democratic countries.

It can happen, of course, that your beard is concealing some imperfection such as a scar or receding chin. Try polling your friends and relatives on the subject by simply removing the beard – temporarily at least.

In the end, the choice should rest on your comfort and friendly feelings toward yourself. While it may be desirable to modify certain unhelpful mannerisms, this does not apply to the face you put forward, which is nothing less than a projection of yourself. After all, your objective should be to feel at ease with other people. And, no matter what the others think, that alone should guide your decision.

Where there is smoke

Do you still smoke? Is there an ashtray on your interviewer's desk? What do you do if you are invited to light up 'if you wish'?

Don't do it!

Regrettable though it may be, the invitation might simply be a rather sly test – unless the speaker is also a smoker.

Keep in mind that reformed smokers – as the interviewer may well be – can be the least tolerant. They are very likely to be acutely aware of the dangers of passive smoking. How, then, can you have a constructive chat with someone who feels like your victim?

CHAPTER 5
The quilted wall

Rarely do executives view the need to 'sell themselves' as anything other than a painful experience. They often, in fact, explain their wish to change jobs in a similarly negative fashion: job threatened; lack of promotion opportunity; even 'differences' with management.

One may add that in general few people enjoy being exposed to the judgement of others, especially if they fail to recognise – often with reason – any claim to superiority on the part of their 'judges'.

A further depressing element may become apparent as the search for a new post continues. If the candidate is at all realistic, they understand that the chances are slim that a first meeting is going to lead to a good 'fit'. (My own figures indicate that six out of seven initial interviews will lead nowhere.) This being the case, at least the person might hope to be able to profit from these meetings as a learning experience.

Reasonable as this expectation might be, candidates often find themselves up against a strange phenomenon: each time that they try to find out the reasons for a rejection (assuming that it comes from the employer's side), there is no valid answer. Why does the truth, potentially so useful to the candidate, remain camouflaged behind such phrases as 'You are overly qualified for the post.' (meaning, usually, 'You are too expensive.')?

Others will state that the decision was extremely hard to arrive at. 'You were among the finalists. In the end we chose someone with more overseas experience.' Another common remark is that the rejected candidate was second choice among the applicants. While 'explanations' of this sort may be considered to be 'kind', they are singularly unhelpful. Comforted, the candidate goes off to repeat the same errors, whatever they might be, in the course of future interviews.

At the same time every job searcher encounters openings for which they are clearly not suited – lack of correspondence between your profile and the post, salary not acceptable, poor reports about the company in question. In such cases, you are the person to make the decision and there is nothing hidden in the equation.

These situations do not need any reflection. What you do need to look at are those missed opportunities for which, in fact, you are supremely well qualified, and which promise job satisfaction and a good future. When such possibilities escape you more than once you have no choice but to examine for yourself the reasons for what you perceive to be your 'failure'.

Don't wait for a series of such disappointments to learn why so many employers hide the real reasons for their choice. They often do so because their decision has been based on affinity, stemming from their feelings about the way the person speaks, dresses and behaves: 'He is my kind of guy.' How can they admit to the 'loser' that the job went to someone the interviewer – to put it bluntly – felt good about? They do not give the real reasons because often they themselves don't have answers that are easily defendable. In truth, they simply liked the other candidate and how they came across. To make such a statement to the loser would not only risk being hurtful, but would also open the interviewer to accusations of non-scientific management or following hunches rather than basing decisions on solid fact. So the conspiracy of silence goes on, as it always will when managers are asked to explain the subjective side of their decision making.

You are left with no choice: you must discover the answers for yourself.

I hope you are reading these words at the beginning of your search. It is never too early (nor it is really ever too late) to undertake the tough, even painful task of self-examination into the sensitive matter of how others perceive us. In the very special case of the job interview, let's face it: you are up for judgement and the verdict will probably have a pronounced effect on what happens in the rest of your life. It is well worth the time, trouble and risk of discomfort to 'get it right'.

THE OTHER SIDE OF THE DESK

From my earliest contacts with executives seeking a job change, I have been struck time and again by a curious phenomenon. I now know it is possible, perhaps even probable, that a single individual holding a responsible position can in fact be two utterly distinct people. In one of their roles we see effective executives, at ease with the level of authority they hold, convincing in their arguments and demonstrating the negotiating skills important in moving the company forward – in sum people who deliver good value for the pay they receive. Moreover, this same individual usually has also had the experience of interviewing candidates for their own staff. Yet observe what happens when they move to the other side of the desk to assume the role of job seeker. Suddenly we have a close-up of a person trying without notable success to mask feelings of discomfort – droning on at times about past history, at other times producing seemingly evasive answers to perfectly objective questions and at still other moments bungling salary negotiations without knowing it. In brief, the seasoned manager can now be seen showing all the human relation skills of a teenager.

This is a caricature, of course, but it does make a point. Haven't we all shown, at one time or another, symptoms of unease while being interviewed for a job? Yet how many of us ever pause to ask ourselves – frankly and objectively – certain obvious and basic questions? What is really going on in the job interview to cause so many of us to change our usual behaviour simply because we have moved a few feet from one side of the desk to the other? Why is it that most of us can negotiate far more effectively in the interests of our company, its products and services, than we often can to assure the future well-being of ourselves and our families?

Here are some solutions to these problems.

Premise 1: Companies hire people, not just degrees, CVs and letters of reference

Either some kind of current will pass between you and your interviewer or not. And if that current does not pass very early in your meeting, no amount of wishful thinking after that will bring about a positive outcome.

In this light, the first few minutes – perhaps even the first few seconds – of the meeting become vitally important. I do not intend at this point to go into the widely known details of how to enter a room, how to shake hands, how to choose your clothing and the many other small matters which are probably automatically part of your day-to-day routine. (Except to add a reminder, perhaps unnecessarily, that a smile has yet to be improved upon as a means of relaxing first encounters.)

There are far more fundamental questions of attitude and behaviour to be considered if the contact is to be one of synergy between you and the interviewer. The key question is, how does one achieve, in a situation of potential stress, a feeling of being 'OK', to use a key word from transactional analysis, that useful way, American by origin, of looking at human relations? By the way, we should not get trapped into applying the word 'relaxed' in this context. The job interview is unquestionably an important issue to the people on both sides of the desk. Mutual comprehension is seldom easily come by and requires a certain amount of effort on the part of both people. A meeting that is totally relaxed may well be a meeting that is going nowhere. On the other hand, any reasonable level of tension can be released in animation of the right kind.

Premise 2: The present is the past

Human beings differ – and happily so – in terms of the richness and dynamism of our everyday exchanges. At the same time they share a certain number of common experiences, and this applies particularly to the life histories of business executives and professional people. Underpinning their careers we usually find at least 20 years of personal history, including home training and formal education, which are together responsible for certain indelibly formed habits. More often than not we also find in their past parents who were very much concerned with their child's level of present performance and future status.

That the consequences of such patterns never entirely disappear from our make-up is generally accepted, not only among psychologists but also by most lay people. Indeed, far from being erased, these influences from the past simply lie buried under the weight of acquired knowledge, as well as the impact of whatever behaviour standards are imposed by the society around us. It is no news to most people that certain kinds of events and situations can trigger off the abrupt reappearance of childlike behaviour in adults – a birthday party, a quarrel with a spouse or lover, frustration of all sorts. A prime example of the collapse of 'grown-up' behaviour is the courtroom scene – a Hollywood favourite – in which the witness is reduced by cross-examination to extremes of childish emotion.

Premise 3: The interview is not a cross-examination

Many people unconsciously approach interview situations as a kind of examination of their credentials and their character. The underlying assumption in such a case is that a 'superior' – perhaps a future boss – is intent on grilling an 'inferior' – the candidate – to search out their points of weakness. In other words, we feel, even if obscurely, ourselves to be involved in a particular kind of cross-examination.

The recognition that such a common illusion can in fact exist as a latent part of our mix of attitudes represents a first step, but only a first step, towards removing one of the chief obstacles to ensuring the best possible results from each meeting. You will find it worth while to dig a little deeper into the implications of this and every similar assumption that presupposes the interview to be a kind of joust that is surreptitiously intended to topple you from your mount of self-esteem. (A joust, I might add, in which the other participant's lance always seems to be longer than your own.)

Transactional analysis (TA) is today widely used to improve human relations in both homes and offices, but I find it particularly valuable in the conduct of employment meetings. You needn't be student of TA to make very practical use of one of its basic concepts in a precise and constructive way. Referring as it does to the analysis of everyday transactions between people, TA rests on the assumption that we all carry within our make-up three components of our personality. Each one of these components is ready to swing into action, sometimes unpredictably, in varying circumstances. The one that dominates in any given situation is likely to determine the nature of our inter-change with another person or persons. Here, then, are the three 'building blocks' that are a part of every human transaction.

The adult

When we are able to apply rational, objective reasoning to the analysis and possible solution of problems, we are using the kind of intelligence that is acquired step by step, both through formal education and practical experience – in other words, through the process of maturing. In its application to our way of relating to other people, the Adult can be characterised by the words, 'Come on, let's reason this out together.' There's not much passion in the Adult. Nor is impulsiveness the Adult's hallmark.

The parent

The Parent represents that part of our nature that has absorbed the attitudes, behaviour patterns and injunctions impressed upon us by our own parents. Keep in mind that their influence was greatest during the years when we were most vulnerable. We may not always be able to recall specifically what was said and done during those early formative years. None the less, the emotional imprint remains. We can recognise it at times when we ourselves show tendencies to become authoritarian, controlling, sometimes arbitrary in our dealings with others. Listen out for your use of words like 'should', 'must', 'ought' and indeed 'listen!', but with an exclamation mark.

The child

In a complex industrialised civilisation this impish side of our social functioning can be, and often is, seen as a danger to 'smooth impersonal relations'. The Child is defined by TA as the spontaneous, feeling side of our behaviour. We have already pointed out that our childish impulses can be suppressed to a greater or lesser degree, but without ever really being removed from among the sources of our later behaviour. However, both the Parent and the Adult within us frequently make war on this unpredictable, sometimes disturbing, aspect of our own selves. High achievers in business and the professions show a natural tendency to favour the Adult (reasoning) and Parental (controlling) sides of their nature. Sometimes the regular use of these aspects translates itself into a concerted effort to 'kill' the vagrant, unpredictable Child who is seen as as threat to 'rational' and 'effective' performance. The fact is that no amount of conscious effort can ever really guarantee the eradication of the Child. Indeed, the more its presence is ignored, the more likely it is (as we see in our own children) to 'act up' at unexpected and inconvenient moments. The Child is impulsive, in a word, and can suddenly fly off into unpredictable temper tantrums, self-pity or inexplicable light-hearted fantasy.

In the personality mix of most people there is a built-in tendency to favour one or the other of these three attitudes – but never to the entire exclusion of the other two. Very probably you can think of someone who seems constantly to be giving advice and instructions to others, even to the point of trying to control their actions – in short playing the role of Parent. Others treat every problem, including the most human, as an intellectual exercise in which feelings have no part – their own or the other person's. Such people tend to favour their Adult side, while a third category may be spontaneous and, erratic, sometimes happy, sometimes sad. They act from their feelings, from their inner Child, and often they are found in creative roles.

In the right circumstances, childlike behaviour can be seductively charming; in other situations it can be downright devastating. The sudden emergence of the Child in a group session can turn a serious committee meeting into a verbal brawl without anyone present knowing exactly what happened.

Transactional analysis postulates further that people carry into their transactions with others the sense that they are feeling 'OK' or 'not OK', in other words that they are either feeling generally comfortable with themselves or mostly ill-at-ease. As a result, it is possible to enter into a relationship that is likely to be dominated by any one of the three following combinations of feeling.

1 'I'm OK. You're OK.'
2 'I'm not OK. You're OK.'
3 'I'm OK. You're not OK.'

How do these various states of mind and emotions apply to the subject of the job interview? The answer is very directly. Even a superficial understanding of this psychological chemistry offers you the chance to avoid the trap that lurks in the very nature of employment meetings – and in fact is more responsible for failures than any other single factor. Read on.

Premise 4: The interview can awaken the Child

Unless you are fully aware of the possibility, you can find your communication skills damaged by the fact that the employment interview, due to its interrogatory quality, can strike emotional chords that are remarkably similar to those that frequently characterised the childhood years. These feelings are most likely to be 'not OK', thus setting up the all-too-real possibility of an 'I'm not OK. You're OK.' confrontation.

So, why does this danger exist? The answer is, because of the frequency – say between the ages of 0 and 20 – with which our behaviour is examined and often criticised by people in positions of seemingly almost unlimited superiority and power. Here I refer to parents, school teachers, headmasters, professors and tutors, to mention only a few. These people are usually addicted to posing questions that we sometimes see as being fraught with possibly dire consequences. 'Why are your hands dirty?' 'Why are you late getting home from school?' 'How do you expect to succeed in life if you don't get better grades?'

The how, whys and whats have indeed been a part of our everyday experience, starting even before we have the words to answer back properly. They include questions that can stir uncomfortable feelings of insecurity and anxiety – in other words, 'not OK' feelings. The effects of this type of transaction are reinforced time and again as youngsters add a school environment to their mix of relations. The identical approach that parents use to impose their will also serves the educational system in good stead. 'Children should be seen and not heard' is the usual key. 'I'll ask the questions – *you* had better have the answers.' 'There is a right way and a wrong way of doing things' (this is most often employed when the youngster is doing something wrong).

Of course not all parents and teachers use this kind of one-way communication 'from the top down', any more than all managers always fling orders at their staff. Frequently parent–child relations are marked by a real two-way communication in which the youngster is given a chance to express its feelings and point of view. Since it is a truism that the hierarchy within organisations tends to resemble a family power structure, it is not surprising that people brought up in an atmosphere of some give and take generally find relations with authority less difficult to handle. They have been made to understand that they are persons worthy of respect in their own right and they tend in later years to project 'OK' feelings in business and professional relationships.

But what of the others who, to a greater or a lesser extent, grow up under the more 'classical' system of child-raising? They have their advantages too. Generally, they tend to be results-oriented and highly motivated to prove their worth as adults. From the start they have the idea that hard work, competence and willingness can win both inner and outer recognition, and they stress these qualities in their business, technical or professional lives.

Earlier I suggested that many competent people may lose out in job interviews. Now we are in a position to combine certain elements of past, nearly forgotten influences with more recent, very real accomplishments in order to learn how to transform the interview into a productive communication.

THE THREE TYPES OF EXCHANGES

Perhaps 80 per cent of all candidates fall into the Parent–Child trap without knowing it. The reason for this is that the interview is so commonly seen as a kind of question-and-answer session disturbingly reminiscent of the days when we were grilled by parents and teachers (and were frequently found wanting).

'Why do you wish to leave your present company?' can be interpreted in a similar fashion to such remembered questions as 'Why do you want to drop maths in order to specialise in languages?' (The reason was that you did not do well in mathematics. Is the real reason for your desired change today traceable to some similar kind of weakness?)

Other echoes sound in other typical interview questions: 'Are you really satisfied with the degree of progress you have shown so far in your career?' 'What kind of contribution do you think a person like you could make to our company?' In the course of an ordinary conversation such questions would appear to be perfectly normal. But if the interview is unconsciously felt to be a kind of cross-exmination, the interpretation will be quite different and the interviewee takes a defensive stance. As the applicant gropes for the 'right' answer, the interviewer is already forming the next question which is likely to follow swiftly. Before the interviewee can gauge the other's reaction to the first reply, they are up against another question and the need for another 'right' response.

As this process continues the candidate feels increasingly at a disadvantage and confused, feeling, in short, 'not OK' and seeing no way to climb back into a position of some equality. In rapid order the candidate – a person of competence and control in an executive job – begins to sink into a Parent–Child transaction. The outcome is then all too predictable.

In order to avoid falling into this trap, much – indeed perhaps everything – depends on the tone set at the start of the meeting. This means that, before each interview, you must be prepared to lead the way into a transaction that is other than Parent–Child and, in terms of TA there are only two other possibilities.

1. To establish a Parent–Parent transaction

By now it should be no mystery that people who opt for this type of approach tend to be hard-sell types. Their message is: 'I have learned that your company's figures for the last fiscal year are not what you would like them to be. Something seems to be wrong. I can assure you that I have the ability to turn the situation around if you are prepared to put the problem in my hands.'

The danger here is evident. In effect, a certain division of power between the candidate and the incumbent is proposed. Except, for, or even in the case of, a weak manager, the interviewer is likely to view such a proposition as nothing short of an invasion of some of their own prerogatives. The chances of setting up an abrasive confrontation under such circumstances are all too apparent.

2. To establish an Adult–Adult exchange

At least 90 per cent of the time this option is the right one, avoiding as it does the problems of the Parent–Parent meeting or the Parent–Child encounter. The words Adult–Adult are, in fact, an accurate reflection of the reality of productive job interviews, when relatively senior positions may be involved. On the one side of the desk sits a person representing a company which obviously has certain needs, perhaps concerning future expansion, perhaps to plug a hole in its existing organisation chart or perhaps to overcome a threatening problem. On the other side is an individual possessing certain abilities, backed by an array of education and experience. The objective Adult question then becomes: 'What is the degree of overlap between the needs of the enterprise and the skills the visitor has to offer?'

However, I am not, in recommending the Adult–Adult approach, in any way proposing a frigid, hyper-rational, intellectual encounter. Of course the use of feelings and intuition will always play their part. To be avoided, however, is the triggering of unconscious, 'not OK' feelings that may, once the gates are open, submerge the Adult.

CHAPTER 6

The questioning technique

Based on our discussion so far, we have seen that an underlying objective in interviews is to assure that our Adult remains as fully functional as possible. Only in this way can a productive exchange of information be hoped for.

How, then, do we protect the Adult in a face-to-face session with another person who probably cherishes their habitual Parent-like role? How do we safeguard our emotional, subjective Child from reacting compulsively to a flow of parental-type questions with their echoes of the past? How, more pointedly, do we transform the meeting into an Adult–Adult situation?

We will begin with some rules.

Rule 1 (which may astonish you): Omit the word 'interview' from your vocabulary.

I know that I have been using the word repeatedly. But I have had a reason. Up to now we have been examining attitudes that commonly prevail before I commence any discussion of the subject with my client. In other words the word 'interview' describes the traditional mental image which most people take into pre-employment meetings. It is also a word that is indirectly responsible for many of their failures. If you yourself are bent on succeeding in your own contacts, a good way to start is to look up the word 'interview' in your dictionary. One definition, for example, mirrors the usual feelings associated with pre-employment meetings: 'A meeting for obtaining information by questioning a person or persons…'. A second meaning is: 'A formal meeting in which a person or persons question, consult or evaluate another or others.'

In other words, the interview is clearly defined as a kind of examination and thus is precisely the type of transaction, on the executive level at least, that we have gone to some lengths to warn against.

Putting the matter another way, we can readily visualise the 'interview' as a kind of game of darts in which the 'interviewer' throws questions at the 'interviewee', seemingly with the object of striking points of vulnerability. The interviewee, then, shifts and squirms in order to avoid being struck in spots which might hurt.

By substituting the word 'meeting', even in our thoughts, for the word interview we take the first essential step towards entering each discussion on the right basis. A meeting is an exchange of information and ideas. It is a game of tennis rather than a game of darts. The conversational ball goes back and forth, and as it does so the people involved engage in a process of understanding each other's situation. Put another way, a meeting is by nature an Adult–Adult transaction. The word interview implies all too clearly a Parent–Child transaction.

Rule 2: Keep firmly in mind a great truth which most people overlook in their anxiety to prove themselves 'acceptable'; the person you are talking to is really, at heart, on your side.

Meetings with job candidates can occupy an enormous amount of an executive's time. Of course the final choice can be vital for the future of the company or department. None the less, the hours spent talking with job seekers, who turn out not to be acceptable, represent a serious drain of the executive's attention from other responsibilities. Furthermore, employment meetings by nature are seldom relaxed sessions. A certain tension is almost inevitable and it is followed, more often than not, by a sense of frustration on both sides of the desk whenever a good match does not exist.

For these reasons the interviewer (yes, the word can be used here since most of them probably regard themselves in this role) almost always hopes that the interviewee will turn out to be the solution to the problem, permitting the interviewer to get back to work. The questions may be penetrating, the attitude may often seem rather tough, but this does not alter the basic fact that the interviewer would like to be convinced that you are the person for the job. If you yourself can maintain this perfectly accurate view of the interviewer's motives, you have already come a long way towards ceasing to visualise the meeting as a game of darts with yourself as the target.

Rule 3: Ask questions.

Behind that simple suggestion there are some ramifications which are not always readily understood. You should use your questioning technique to ensure that the conversational ball will indeed pass back and forth between you and your interviewer. Because of the engrained ideas that most of us bring into any meeting called a 'job interview', the proper use of this technique requires a new way of thinking and, especially, of feeling. It means that we must break certain conditioned reflexes that may be firmly in control as a combined result of our early conditioning and of conventional wisdom (which, after all, is simply an amalgam of individual experience and 'wisdom').

So, there are habit patterns that need to be broken and then to be replaced by a new set of reflexes. This may sound a formidable task at first, but in fact what I am recommending is perfectly normal executive behaviour in many other circumstances. Once again the problem is our own conception of how a pre-employment meeting is to be handled! Before this is entirely tamed, you may require two or three meetings to perfect your own questioning technique. (Or, if you are working with a qualified career counsellor, you have the opportunity to sharpen your skill with their help.)

So how, you may ask at the outset, it is possible to pose a lot of questions under such circumstances without either seeming cheeky or appearing to probe into matters that are really the interviewer's business? The dilemma is more apparent than real. There is a key and here it is: The questions *you* pose should, for the most part, be linked to the questions the other person puts to you. You need to have your mind on two things at once. One part of your mind frames the answer to the interviewer's question while simultaneously a second part should be busy with the following: 'What question does this particular question bring to mind?'

In Chapter 7 you will find 11 commonly asked questions. The answers I suggest show clearly how your replies can indeed be linked directly to the other person's question, thus giving the interviewer the comfortable feeling of being in charge of the proceedings, while at the same time producing important benefits for yourself.

1 The responses to your questions will provide you with valuable, even necessary, information about the company, the position and the person you are talking to. Never forget that your best potential source of information about a company is not its annual report, nor the analysis of stock evaluation services, but rather a person involved in its affairs on a meaningful level, in other words, very probably the person seated across from you.

2 While your interviewer is replying to your questions, you have a breather. You have given yourself time to reflect on the evolution of the meeting thus far, to think ahead and to better tune your mind to that of the interviewer.

3 You have now probably moved the transaction from a potential Parent–Child exchange to an Adult–Adult communication. The

'tennis game' is under-way; the ball is passing back and forth. You begin to be seen by the other person in an executive role, as an individual fully competent to handle negotiations from the other side of the desk.

In order to illustrate the use of the questioning technique more accurately, we will look at your possible response to one of the many questions you are probably being asked. This sample will allow you to compare your own usual answer with our recommended reply.

Since it is not unusual for your interviewer to be concerned with matters of forward planning and timing, one question may go like this:

'You realise, of course, Mr Smith, that this is our first meeting and that no firm decision will be made today. None the less, if we were to make an offer to you later – and if you decided to accept – in this case, how long would it be before you would be free to take up the post?'

In my experience at least 80 per cent of the job seekers I talk to will reply to this question with some kind of time estimate, yet it takes little reflection to see that there is actually no correct answer. If you say 'I can make it as soon as you wish' you are saying that:

1 you are an 'unemployed drain on the job market';
2 that you are ready to leave an employer without regard to the needs of your present company; or
3 that your present company will be glad to see you go, and the sooner the better.

On the other hand, if you project an important delay you may be walking into another trap. The company may be hoping to fill the spot quickly and the next candidate greeting the receptionist may be highly qualified, out of work for honourable reasons and immediately available.

As is often the case, a questioning attitude can save you from falling into either of these traps. Instead of replying with an answer, why not pose a question yourself? Your reply might well be:

'I am able to be flexible in the matter. But, tell me, what is your own timing? How soon do you wish to fill the post?'

The answer you get will give you important information. If the need turns out to be urgent, you can deal with it on that basis. However, you may be facing a situation involving a reorganisation that could take months to complete. Here your negotiating position is quite different; you would have weakened your case unnecessarily by being too readily available.

Regardless, however, of your interviewer's reply, it is better not to try to be specific. You can continue the conversation by saying:

'Of course, I am involved right now in a number of personal and business considerations, including certain negotiations I have under way. I'd rather not give an offhand answer to your question. But I am certain I could sort matters out in 48 hours. If you agree, I will plan to telephone you on Wednesday morning with a more precise reply.'

If you get agreement to this suggestion, you now have established a re-entry by telephone into the interviewer's office. One important aspect of this general technique is to seek out every opportunity – with their assent, of course – to get back in touch with the interviewer. In this particular case, you will have no problem with your contact's secretary to whom you will be able to say, 'I am phoning as agreed with Mr Martin'. If, on the contrary, your suggestion is shrugged off, you have still gained, since you have not committed yourself in a way that could block the progress of the meeting. At the same time you have made it clear that you have other prospects in the offing without hammering home the point.

This is only one example, but a good one, of how the questioning technique can help lead you towards a firm offer through the simple process of keeping the door open to that possibility.

Rule 4: You are there to win.

Does that sound obvious? Well, the answer is yes and no. There is a 'not OK' devil inside many of us who whispers 'Let's reject the interviewer before I am rejected'. In the case of employment meetings this self-protective attitude can masquerade behind subtle guises: 'I'm not sure this is my kind of person', 'I don't like his beard' or 'Really, this is a pretty crummy office'. This subtle invasion of negative signals may well have a self-defeating psychological motivation. We feel that our ego is to some extent on the line at every employment meeting. If we can find a few reasons – valid or not – why 'this is not the job for me', the threat of rejection is automatically averted. How can you fail to win a tawdry prize that you never really tried to win in the first place? Thus the ego may emerge from such a meeting in grand shape' the only drawback is that your job search has not been advanced in the least. Even worse, the opportunity to use that meeting as a positive experience has been lost because you haven't even tried to play the game.

Every statement about employment meetings has to be tempered because of the nuances that result from the infinite differences between people and between the situations they face. I am not suggesting that you chase every useless opportunity to the bitter end. Clear, objective reasoning will sometimes tell you that a given job is not for you, and why. If, however, your lack of motivation is simply based on 'hunch', 'sixth sense' or 'feel', you should question yourself rather closely. As for myself, when one of my clients reports back after five or six successive meetings to the effect that each job 'wasn't for me', I begin to ask pointed questions and to listen very carefully to the reasons why my client's job campaign may be heading for the rocks.

Rule 5: Beware of the CV.

In fact, I suggest you leave your CV at home.

This document may, of course, have preceded you in certain situations, particularly if your contact with the prospective employer was arranged by an executive search firm or a recruiting agency. Whenever possible, however, you are well advised to avoid allowing this piece of paper to intrude between you and your interviewer. We have talked at some length about the importance of establishing an Adult basis of communication. To hand over your CV on the spot may, in the candidate's eyes, be a very objective and therefore 'Adult' action ('After all, it's facts that make objectivity and my CV is nothing but'). Unfortunately, your motives for handing over a CV without being asked can be open to question from the outsider. It is entirely possible that your CV will be seen as a kind of crutch you are using to support a weakness in carrying on a frank and open discussion.

Secondly, there is the real risk of breaking direct face-to-face communication early in your meeting – perhaps at the very moment when it is vital for you to be building a bridge of mutual understanding. Finally, the interviewer can always find your CV a convenient way to take full control of the discussion. In this case, the interviewer will pluck items here and there from your history, demanding explanations and amplifications, while checking the consistency of your replies. With such a scenario scripting your meeting, you may well find it impossible even to start to discuss your real qualifications in the light of the particular needs of the interviewer's organisation. There is one simple reason for this. You may never learn what those needs are; time has run out.

On the other hand, consider the merits of telling the interviewer that you will gladly send a CV which you are completing. You then score three advantages. First, you have kept open the path to direct verbal communication. Secondly, you grant yourself the opportunity to target your CV to that particular job. And thirdly, by sending the CV in the post, you have established another re-entry into the interviewer's office. The interviewer is forced to remember you, your face, your situation, while other candidates are beginning to fade. From your own experience in the role of interviewer, you may recall how hard it is to keep names and faces sorted out after a few days of such meetings.

So, your CV sent out after your meeting confirms and reinforces a good contact. It does not take control of what should be a direct and human interchange of information.

CHAPTER 7

The proactive negotiator

Everything that has been said up to this point is intended to indicate that your success or failure in pre-employment negotiations depends almost as much on how you present your qualifications as on the merits of the qualifications themselves.

Because we rightly see ourselves as unique individuals – one of a kind, beyond all doubt – we tend to carry our thinking further, and to expect that the wide and varied world of business and the professions will certainly contain one or more opportunities corresponding to our particular array of experiences and competences. By extension, then, aren't we justified in viewing the meeting with a prospective employer as a simple matter of listening to their description of an available position and then replying to their questions?

Based on what you have read so far, you already know that I do not regard the job 'interview' in this light. The person who adopts this approach in a search for new opportunities is typical of the vast majority of executives faced with the need or the desire to make a change. I have come to call this way of exploring the job market the 'reactive' approach. One sure sign of the reactive approach is the tendency of many people to react to an interesting job advertisement by rushing to the post-box to be sure that their reply is among the first to be opened. Such people do not reflect on the fact that 80 per cent of their competitors react in the same way, whereas a letter posted a few days later stands to receive far greater attention as the first flood of replies begins to recede. Likewise:

- *reactive people* wait for executive search firms to contact them rather than taking the initiative to make their availability known to the firms in a direct and positive way;
- *reactive people* are sure that their friends and contacts will make important efforts on their behalf without their finding a concrete way to motivate them to do so;
- *reactive people* will slow down their efforts to make new contacts whenever a hopeful negotiation is under way for an interesting position, rather than to continue to seek out new possibilities.

In using the words proactive and reactive, I am metamorphizing the terms from transactional analysis – 'the Adult' and 'the Child' – into a more businesslike terminology. But the sense of the words remains exactly the same.

There is nothing either unusual or blameworthy in a reactive approach. Its sole negative aspect is its ineffectiveness. We are certainly justified in our conviction that there exists somewhere in the world of work the right place for the best use of our talents and skills. What many people fail to realise is that the best of such opportunities may lie forever beyond our grasp, unless we ourselves generate a positive, creative approach to seeking them out.

I call this way of attacking the job search the proactive approach. The word proactive is a useful addition to the English language. All other words intended to describe the opposite of reactivity turn out to be misleading in the context of the conduct of negotiations in one's own self-interest. We are not, for example, recommending aggression with its implication of bared fangs. Nor does the word energetic quite fit the bill, since energy either can be wisely directed or scattered. Proactivity, in the sense that I use the word, simply suggests that our actions are controlled by our own initiative rather than stemming from the initiative of others. Outside the job search examples of reactive behaviour in companies abound.

- The person who always waits for management to offer them a salary increase or promotion, rather than seeking ways to bring about a change.
- The person who may be asked to lunch with colleagues but hesitates to ask them back.
- The person who consistently performs jobs assigned to them without seeking new tasks that need doing.

Thus the choice of whether to be reactive (the Child) or proactive (the Adult) presents itself every day in every situation, from the question of who first greets whom, to matters of marriage and divorce, or whether to buy or sell investments.

In few situations do these two frames of mind show themselves more clearly than in the job interview.

You will find among the following questions some that are nearly always posed in such selection meetings. Others you will probably encounter at one time or another. My concern, however, is not with the frequency with which you are confronted by these examples. Even if you never meet any of them, you will still benefit from the principle behind the framing of the suggested responses. In each case I have given typical responses to each question cited: the 'classical' or reactive reply, followed by the response framed in a proactive way.

THE OPENING GAMBITS

Earlier I mentioned the important role of non-verbal communications in ensuring effective human contacts. Now we are directly concerned with the words you choose to use.

It is useful at this point to repeat once more the crucial character of the first few minutes of the meeting. The opening exchanges may well determine the tone of your entire meeting. For this reason you must be very aware of the need to respond constructively to any early questions that represent any kind of potential trap. In using this word, I do not mean that the other person is deliberately laying a trap for you, rather that you risk trapping yourself as a result of an overly impulsive response.

Certain questions that arise before you have had enough time to establish good communications are to be handled with particular care. If, at this get-acquainted stage, you produce black-and-white answers contrary to what the interviewer wants or expects, you can be put at more of a disadvantage than from the same reply given once a good rapport has been established.

To illustrate this point, let us assume that the interviewer has just emerged from a meeting on the subject of the company's finances. Thinking about the problem of costs the interviewer loses no time getting around to the question of your salary level. Here we have a good example of several questions to which there is likely to be no right answer. Whatever salary level you name is liable to be either higher or lower than the one the interviewer has in mind. Yet you know instinctively that any attempt to 'bargain' at this early stage may side-track your meeting into a dangerous blind alley.

A person using the reactive approach is likely to try to solve the dilemma something like this:

'To my mind salary is not as important as finding a really satisfying job with good future growth. However, it may be helpful to you to know that my present salary level is £35 000 per year.'

A proactive approach, on the other hand, will produce an answer more like this:

'Of course the question of salary is important to both of us. However, at this point I have very little knowledge of the position under discussion. If you have no objection I'd like to hear more details, after which I'll be glad to take up the matter of compensation.'

Objectively speaking, this is a perfectly reasonable stance and will usually be regarded as such. If, as may happen on rare occasions, the other person continues to bulldoze away on the salary question you may be receiving useful signals concerning the financial situation of the company.

Another potentially delicate point during the opening gambits is the matter of who imparts information first. Sometimes a meeting with a company will open with the interviewer putting before you a fairly complete outline of the specifications of the vacant post. When this is the case, the candidate starts off with an obvious advantage. Unfortunately, this open-handed approach is not always encountered, often because the organisation itself has not yet clearly defined the profile of the person it is searching for. In such situations, the candidate may be flying dangerously blind at the start of the meeting.

Here is how best to deal with such 'blind' starts. Skilled and unskilled interviewers alike will often begin the conversation in a similar fashion – the latter because they do not know a better way, the former because their question helps them learn much about the interviewees' ways of thinking. The opening question in either case might go like this:

'As a way of starting the meeting, I suggest you simply tell me about yourself in your own words.'

REACTIVE RESPONSE 1: *'I grew up in Oxford and went to school in the city. After leaving school, I was accepted by the University of Bristol where I graduated in economics. My first job in 1976 was as a trainee with British Steel ...'*

REACTIVE RESPONSE 2: *'My career has been primarily in technical sales and I am presently north-east area manager for No-Glitch Computers. Before joining No-Glitch I was product manager for Wiseacre Calculators ...'*

Reactive response 2 is much more effective than the first reactive response simply because it deals with a question of immediate interest: 'What are you doing right now?' Reactive response 1, on the other hand, flirts with two risks at the same time. The most dangerous one is that of pure boredom. Your early days in Oxford have about as much relevance to the interviewer as the adventures of Red Riding Hood. The interviewer is busy and no doubt a person dealing with a variety of immediate problems. If you are going to say things that are not interesting, you can almost count on the fact that the interviewer's mind will detach itself to deal with more stimulating matters. 'Is the insurance on the Beacon warehouse sufficient?' 'What did the boss mean when he spoke about setting new corporate objectives?'

Most executives have some skill at dissembling and your interviewer is probably no exception. You won't know that they are not really listening because of their alert expression and occasional 'Yes' and 'I see'. In brief you have lost contact without knowing it.

A second risk – less likely perhaps but even more dangerous in using the historical approach is the possibility that you may never have a chance at all to talk about the present and the competences you possess today. Digressions ('Oh, you come from Oxford. Do you happen to know Bob Smith? He must be about your age.') or telephone interruptions can quickly eat up the time allotted. The words, 'So sorry, but our time seems to have run out' can come just as you are launching into describing your present, and most relevant, position.

A PROACTIVE RESPONSE: *'Of course I am glad to give you any information about myself you may wish. You have received my CV and my letter, and you seem to have found some points of interest in it that promoted this meeting. May I suggest we use one of these as a starting point. Could you tell me which of those points interest you the most?'*

You have now set in motion the important business of learning what the other person is looking for. The reply, for example, may be: 'I see you've had experience in the selection and training of exclusive sales agents. Tell me more about that.' If so, you have some immediate insight into the needs of the company, as well as assurance that what you are about to say is on target. In discussing any single aspect of your career, set yourself an absolute limit of three minutes of monologue. Then interrupt yourself, saying (for example), 'I have also installed and managed an effective sales incentive programme for our own direct sales people. Would you like to hear about that aspect of my work?'

The interviewer's response – positive or negative – carries along a process of defining the fit between the company's needs and your own experience. Furthermore, you are setting up a series of checks to make sure that what you are saying is geared to the other person's interest.

The basic principle is that you should always make every effort to find out what the other person's situation is. This is simply good salespersonship, well known, for example, to the door-to-door seller of vacuum cleaners. Once in the target's living room the salesperson is not likely to chat about the superb steel from Zaïre that went into the product or the quality control system at the factory. More probably the salesperson will be scrutinising the room, searching for dog hairs on the carpet, dust on the curtains or cigarette ash on the floor. Then the salesperson will say 'I see you have a pet. Let me show you how fast the Superclean can dispose of dog hairs with no effort whatsoever on your part.'

At this point you may object that not all interviewers will co-operate in your efforts to get them to show their dog hairs. Some of them may very well insist that you talk about yourself 'in your own way'. Even so, you have lost nothing by showing your knowledge of good negotiating skills. If the other person does insist on sticking to their structure, you obviously are not going to persist. In this case, simply give your story succinctly, concentrating on your present job and on some of the results you have obtained. You should focus more on the competences and knowledge that you presently possess than on historical data.' Even a child has had 'experience'. The question to be dealt with in a 'potted history' is how that history might be turned to the practical advantage of the employer.

This first volley does not need to last more than three or four minutes. At the end, come in with a question, such as: 'That's a brief panorama of my background. Tell me, which aspect would you like to hear more about?' In this way you have met the apparent need of the interviewer to do things their way, but at the same time you have taken a step back in your own efforts to get a sense of the direction of the interviewer's thoughts. If you are successful you will reap dividends later when the question may be floated: 'Ideally, what kind of position are you looking for?'

At this point the value of understanding the other person's requirements becomes clear. To illustrate, here are some typical reactive and proactive responses.

A REACTIVE RESPONSE: *'I see myself best situated in sales management, preferably in an international company such as yours.'*

A PROACTIVE RESPONSE: *'My goal is to join a company with a product line similar to yours, and I hope the position will stress both sales and marketing management. Ideally there would be emphasis on setting up, training and motivating sales teams, opening up new markets and selecting and training distributors and agents.'*

Without being in possession of specific information about the requirements and plans of the company, you obviously cannot be so specific in your reply. You might risk being dangerously off the mark. The dilemma is illustrated by the reactive response cited: it is necessarily bland and generalised and gives the probably false impression that you have not come to grips with your own future objectives.

The proactive response, on the other hand, incorporates specific information you have gleaned from your opening exchanges, provided, of course, that the elements named are part of a job you really want to have and are convinced you can do. In other words, if you have learned that the company is seeking a chief pencil-sharpener, I am hardly suggesting that you include this chore as a part of your ideal job description ... unless, of course, you really do have a thing about sharpening pencils.

In fact, nothing in these pages is suggesting that you warp the facts, either about your past history or your future goals. It is all too easy to become confused on this point. Proactivity in handling 'interviews' does not simply mean loose playing with the truth. What it does mean is that you project the facts in the most constructive way possible. With this in mind, we will now go on to examine further typical 'trap questions'.

CHAPTER 8

Early 'trap questions'

I have already stressed the importance of the first tone-setting minutes. This statement applies to a wide variety of human contacts. While real communication is in the process of being established, people tend instinctively to avoid sensitive subjects. Perhaps that is the fundamental reason for the existence of small talk, such as discussions of the weather. For some engineers, scientists and technical people, exchanges of this kind can be almost painful. They often have trouble seeing the value of such a 'waste of time'. Salespeople and general managers, however, tend to play the game. They understand that even a small insight into the other person's way of seeing things is going to help comunications when conversation moves on to matters of greater substance.

For the most part, the use of small talk is not likely to characterise the start of employment meetings. As a result, important subjects may arise swiftly with no preparation of common ground. In such a typical situation, applicants who respond to direct questions in a reactive way are likely to find themselves at a particular disadvantage.

Let me emphasise again that the words 'trap questions' should not be interpreted to mean that the other person has deliberately set a trap. It is quite possible for people to trap themselves. The interviewer simply listens and reaches certain judgements. If these judgements are negative, the meeting will go on in a seemingly normal manner, but in the mind of the other person the candidate is already not the 'right solution' to the organisational problem being faced.

Study the following examples of reactive and proactive responses to questions that can represent either 'traps' or bridges that may lead to a positive outcome.

QUESTION: *'Tell me, what are your longer range career objectives? For example, where do you see yourself ten years from now?'*

A REACTIVE RESPONSE: *'I feel that I can make a sufficient contribution to the company to occupy a key position in general management.'*

A PROACTIVE ANSWER: *'My objective quite simply is to progress as far in the management of a company such as this as my own abilities and energies will carry me. Naturally, I am interested to hear from you how you view the possible future evolution from this position.'*

Behind the words   Question such as this, having to do with long-range objectives, have implications on a level of feelings for the questioner as well as for the applicant. The person you are talking to may well be older than you. When the interviewer's mind leaps ahead ten years what does the interviewer see? Retirement? Blockage? We cannot assume that a big desk, three telephones and two secretaries spell security. In fact, these props, along with a good title, may be necessary boosters to a person who is trying to prove something as a substitute for being in possession of real feelings of self-confidence.

The reactive response above may arouse unpleasant future vistas for the interviewer by automatically raising questions about their own evolution. This reactive reply, in other words, carries within it a potential threat to the interviewer because you are setting yourself up as one more competitor for future top jobs. None of these vibrations is outwardly expressed, of course. But they may be there and they form a lurking, hidden trap for you. Your answer, instead of coming across as you intended, demonstrating confidence in yourself and your future, can be received in quite another sense: that of diminishing prospects for the older person.

As to the suggested proactive response, the second part should by now be seen as fundamental to the approach I am recommending. In asking how the interviewer sees the evolution from the post in question, you send the conversational ball back to the server in the hope of gaining an insight into the realistic future prospects. But the fundamental idea behind your reply is to make it clear that:

1 you do indeed have a certain ambition and high level of motivation; and
2 your spirit of competition is directed to turning out the best job you are capable of without implying the elbowing aside of others in the process.

THE QUESTION: *Exactly what kind of a contribution do you think you could make to our company?*

A REACTIVE RESPONSE: *'Without any doubt I have the competence and experience to boost your sales and profits substantially.'*

A REACTIVE RESPONSE FROM A FINANCIAL MANAGER: *'With my skills in cost control, I am certain I can bring about operating savings that would have a very positive effect on earnings.'*

A PROACTIVE RESPONSE: *'My way of coming to grips with new situations is to ask questions at the beginning, and to observe the people and the problems until I feel I have a sound understanding of the major factors in play. I believe that specific actions should be based on that kind of knowledge. For the moment the best answer I can give you is to tell you about some of the results I've had in the past.* [Cites three pertinent result histories.] *Do you feel that this kind of approach has value in the situations your company is facing?'*

Behind the words: Far from being hidden, the trap in this question is highly visible. Actually the question is impossible to answer in a direct way simply because you do not have enough information to deal with it. Nor is there any possibility of amassing the necessary facts within the time limit of a single conversation. Recognising this, many candidates simply shy away from the question like a horse facing a high fence. Either they fumble for a reply, with a resulting loss of composure, or they settle for a reply that is so generalised as to be meaningless. A third kind of reactive response is even more dangerous. This is to attempt the impossible by outlining a detailed approach to a situation without having any real bed-rock of knowledge.

In this connection, I should add a word of warning against a particular technique used by a limited number of companies. This practice is to suggest to the candidate that they write down and send their suggestions in as to how they would deal with a particular situation or problem. There was one American multinational company that was about to introduce worldwide a new line of men's cosmetics. In each market, they first advertised an opening for a 'Top Marketing Manager, Consumer Products'. After eliminating in first meetings the persons with the least experience, they invited a handful of qualified candidates to submit their ideas of how to launch the product in their national market. Most were seduced by the prospect of a high salary with interesting growth potential, and they put hours of thought and effort into their presentations in order to 'win' the competition. In the end, the job was never filled by an outside candidate, but the 'employer' gained thousands of dollars worth of creative suggestions at virtually no cost to themselves.

I have never seen an executive hired as a result of a written statement of opinions on how to deal with a situation faced by the prospective employer.

THE QUESTION: *'Your present company has a fine reputation in its field and I understand it is turning out very good operating results. Frankly, I'm having some trouble understanding why you are planning to leave.'*

A REACTIVE RESPONSE: *'At the time I was hired, Noglitch took on many other young trainees – more than they really required. Now many of us find ourselves blocked in terms of future progress.'*

A PROACTIVE RESPONSE: *'You are quite right about Noglitch. It is a fine company. Clearly I would not want to leave except for an unusually good opportunity. That's why I am interested in learning all I can today about the situation you have open.'*

Behind the words The reactive response above raises more questions than it answers. Why did some of the trainees seem to find a good future for themselves, while this candidate seems to be blocked? Why is the candidate showing such motivation to go elsewhere without seriously weighing up the concrete alternatives? Is the candidate in fact in the process of being pushed out of the company?

The proactive response, on the other hand, says that you are weighing one factual situation (your present job) against another factual situation (the specific possibilities that may be open to you elsewhere, before making a decision to move. This is an objective, 'Adult' and pragmatic approach to problem solving. It also says to your interviewer that you value your present job and will not settle for an inferior offer. In short, you are placing yourself on the buyers' market rather than the sellers' market.

If you are without a job, the questioning may take quite a different tack.

THE QUESTION: *'How long have you been out of a job?'*

A REACTIVE RESPONSE: *'About four months.'*

A PROACTIVE RESPONSE: *'I have been actively searching for a period of four months. Several possibilities have come up, but I am determined to accept only a position that makes sense in terms of my overall career. Do you feel this is an intelligent procedure, or would you advise me to settle for an interim situation while looking for something better?'*

Behind the words Everyone likes to give advice, especially people who find themselves in a Parental role. On the other hand, the reactive response above is one that is likely to open a series of questions stated or unstated. Why have you been 'unacceptable' for so long? Are you really trying to solve your employment problem – or just going through the motions? If you have no other good possibilities, does the interviewer want to hire someone who has been turned down so often?' They may think that you could be manipu-lated on questions of salary and other benefits. In contrast to this particular candidate's now-weakened position, the proactive negotiator demon-strates that they are an acceptable product and that they have sufficient character not to settle too quickly for a second-best job. The question at the end of the reply establishes also that the proac-tive candidate is not bull-headed and respects the opinion of a per-son who can regard the situation from a more objective point of view.

THE QUESTION: *'How do you feel about the possibility of changing your place of residence?'*

A REACTIVE RESPONSE: *'For several reasons, my wife and I are not able to consider leaving this area.'*

A SECOND REACTIVE RESPONSE: *'I am absolutely free to move. No prob-lem."*

A PROACTIVE RESPONSE: *'I do have some flexibility in the matter. But what do you have in mind?'*

Behind the words   I have seen serious mistakes made when the applicant assumed the intention of the company. The interviewer's question may be general, it may imply a move to the location where the meeting is being held or it may indicate the possibility of a post far removed either from your home or from the company's headquar-ters. You owe it to yourself to get this clarification if the question is stated in such general terms as above.

Keep in mind that many companies, particularly a number that are US based, have fixed ideas on the subject of an executive's willing-ness to move. I have known several situations where a person's prospects for future advancement within a company were ended with a first or second refusal of a relocation. If the meeting in question is taking place with such a company, your negative response will mean that you have 'trapped' yourself and that, in terms of prac-tical results, the conversation will lead nowhere.

On the other hand, the second reactive response, stating that you will go anywhere, also has its danger. You are, in effect, offering to write a blank cheque on the future both of yourself and your family. There are many locations that are simply not acceptable to an intel-ligent person who cares about the future. You have cheapened yourself in your desire to keep open communication with your interviewer. The question is, how do you achieve the same result more constructively?

First, let us assume that the other person answers your proactive question above with some precision.

THE QUESTION: *'Our company has made numerous studies concerning cost-effective locations for our headquarters. Since the reception of visitors is not an important factor, we have decided to move our communications centre to Tierra del Fuego. How do you feel about such a move?'*

A REACTIVE RESPONSE: *'I'm sorry but I can't stand cold weather and I am not sure that penguins make the best companions.'*

A PROACTIVE RESPONSE: *'I really know very little about Tierra del Fuego, and this raises a point about the relocation policy of your company. Do you make it a practice to send a couple to look over a prospective site before they are expected to commit themselves firmly? I'm speaking here of housing possibilities, educational facilities, quality of life and so forth.'*

Behind the words   Note that this suggested proactive reply is worded in such a way that it avoids any hint of a personal request that you and your spouse receive a free trip from the company. Rather you are asking about the company's general policy in such matters. The response you'll receive can take several forms. The other person may react rather sharply, saying: 'You seem to have some rather radical ideas on management. Our company is in business to make a profit and would not be interested in investing in junkets of that kind.'

An opposite type of response will reveal the intelligent concern of an enterprise to make certain that both spouses are in accord before undertaking a projected move. Such companies know that large investments in moving families have often gone down the drain because of one partner's discontent in the new situation. Such a company may well have a policy like the one the proactive candidate mentions.

Most likely, since this is a first meeting, the other person will reply along the following lines: 'It may be a bit soon to cross that particular bridge. We can come back to the subject later once we establish the degree of mutual interest that may exist between us.'

Regardless of which of the three responses the interviewer chooses, you have learned something about the company's management style and you have not shut the door to further discussion.

THE QUESTION: *'We're starting to touch on some interesting points. Would you have any objection if I asked Mr Martin to join our meeting?'*

A REACTIVE RESPONSE: *'None at all. He is very welcome.'*

A PROACTIVE RESPONSE: *'None at all. But tell me, what is Mr Martin's role in your organisation?'*

Behind the words   Any third or fourth person coming into a pre-employment meeting poses new problems for the candidate. Not only is there bound to be a shifting of psychological transactions, but there is also the simple fact that more people usually mean more and more varied questions for you to deal with. The problem is compounded if you do not know the position of each person in the room. If Mr Martin turns out to be the founder of the company, you will want to address a large part of your attention to him. On the other hand, he may be an assistant to the interviewer, in which case your concentration will probably remain largely focused on your host.

The essential point is never to be caught in the position of not knowing to whom you are talking.

Having dealt well with the opening gambits as well as the early trap questions, you are now very likely to be regarded as an acceptable candidate as the conversation proceeds into the heart of the meeting. The next step is to secure your position of strength.

CHAPTER 9

The follow-through

We can assume that your proactive responses early in your meeting have helped establish a good quality of communication between you and your interviewer. Your non-verbal communication has been positive, you have said nothing to 'turn off' the other person and at the same time you have shown some ability in interpersonal trans-actions. The way is now clear for you to move into a new phase of proactivity. Our discussion up to this point has repeatedly portrayed the interviewer as the source of initiative in the posing of questions. True, the applicant has repeatedly made proactive responses, but always in the role of 'follow-the-leader'. Our next step is to discuss questions that you can and should work into the conversation at appropriate points.

USEFUL QUESTIONS

It is a good thing to have certain questions already in your mind before the start of your meeting. You can readily frame for yourself a number of questions to do with your specific areas of knowledge: sales, finance or engineering, for example. In addition, however, the following suggested questions are intended to ferret out information that you will need in reaching any judgement about a company and its policies.

'To whom does the job report?'

This is a point of vital importance and unfortunately one that is sometimes overlooked. If the person before you is not a personnel manager, you may naturally assume that you are facing your future boss. As some applicants have later found, to their profound regret, this is not necessarily the case. I recall one situation where a mar-keting manager was hired by the managing director of a firm manu-facturing hand tools. When he showed up for work, he learned that he was to report to the sales manager who had had no voice in the selection process. Regarded as a lesson in the danger of making hasty assumptions, the experience may have been useful to my client, but not surprisingly he soon found himself unable to cope with the demands of what were, in effect, two bosses.

'Is the position one that already exists or is it a newly-created post?'

If the post is a new one, you will want to follow through with a number of questions about the objectives to be obtained and the means to be provided to meet them. If, on the other hand, the position already exists, you may well ask the following question.

'What became of the person who held the job?'

There are three possible rejoinders. They may have resigned, been fired or been promoted. If the last answer is the one you receive, you have good evidence that the job may offer an opening for future progress. The other two possible replies will no doubt raise further questions in your mind. However, your sense of diplomacy may well signal that you should not try to probe too deeply.

'I would be glad if you could show me exactly where the post is situated on your organisation chart.'

While your immediate superior is no doubt your most important power relationship, you may well find it useful in judging the status of a position to see it in relation to the entire executive hierarchy. An examination of the chart will also frequently reveal the existence of dotted-lines relationships (with all the potential for ambiguity they imply).

'Is it the usual practice of your company to fill vacant posts from within the organisation or do you customarily recruit from the outside?'

This question may help you to smoke out a situation – not at all unusual – in which a company is conducting a 'beauty contest' between outside candidates and one or more candidates who are already on the staff. People seeking a new post frequently overlook the fact that their chief competition may come from inside, not outside, the organisation. Sometimes, indeed, the matter has already been decided in favour of the insider; the outsider is in fact struggling to obtain a position that is actually no longer vacant.

How can this be? I have seen more than one situation where the managing director had already made a decision in favour of a member of the existing team, even before beginning to arrange meetings with outsiders. The motivation in looking outside is as old as the invention of the limited liability corporation – self-protection. To forestall any possible charges – whether from the board or colleagues – of acting out of favouritism, the MD declares an 'open competition': 'Let the best person win'. An executive search firm is hired, perhaps backed up by newspaper ads describing the post available. Two dozen of the best-qualified candidates are brought in for interviews. All of the proper motions are gone through. The predictable aspect of this particular brand of 'open competition' is that the inside candidate always seems to be the winner. However, in announcing the decision, the MD is on firm ground: 'After conducting an extension search for the best candidate available – whether inside or outside the company – I am glad to announce that Bob Smith of our Lampshade Division Marketing Team has been chosen for the post.'

This kind of deception abounds, especially in the engagement of executives for posts with governmental agencies and educational institutions, which often are required by regulation to advertise the existence of vacancies outside.

From the standpoint of the rejected outside candidate, they must understand that such situations often exist. They did not 'miss out in the competition'; it never existed in the first place.

THE OPENING OF SALARY NEGOTIATIONS

Though you may have been successful in postponing a premature discussion of your salary requirements, as suggested earlier, the subject is almost certain to resurface later on in your meeting.

I am assuming that by now you have a good understanding of the post and have absorbed some knowledge of the company's situation, as well as of future growth possibilities. To make the start of the negotiation as difficult as possible, I am also going to assume that there has been no intervention by an executive search firm and thus no prior knowledge on either side of the desk of the other person's position on the matter.

QUESTION A: *'What is your present salary level?'*

QUESTION B: *'What level of compensation are you seeking?'*

A reactive response to Question A is to give a precise salary figure.

A proactive response You can hardly expect to manipulate your way out of replying to such a direct question. You have, however, the possibility of replying, not in terms of your precise salary, but rather in terms of your total package. If you do so, you must be careful not to use the word 'salary' in framing your reply. Refer instead to your 'compensation'. This permits you to add to your gross salary a sum that approximates the annual value of any fringe benefits you receive. For example, you can readily calculate the yearly worth of your use of a company car, Life insurance premiums paid by the company, stock option plans, major private medical coverage – all of these, plus other perks – are part of your 'compensation'. In no sense, however, should you mislead the interviewer. Your reply thus could take the following form:

'In terms of my total package of compensation, the figure comes to just over £40 000 per year.'

Very few interviewers – particularly in first interviews – ask for a breakdown of the figure you give. However, you have to be prepared for this to happen and your reply must be one that can readily be defended.

A REACTIVE RESPONSE TO QUESTION B: *'I would expect a salary between £30,000 and £40,000 per year.'*

A PROACTIVE RESPONSE: *'You understand that my chief interest is in the profile of my next post in terms of the job satisfaction it offers, of future growth possibilities and the kind of company I would be joining.'*

Having indicated that you are not rigid in your salary demands, your immediate challenge is to learn from the other person the figure they have in mind. Don't forget that any figure you name is almost certain to be higher or lower than the one the interviewer visualises; the law of averages is, quite simply, against your hitting the mark exactly. You can try to get this information in one of two ways: the first by using a direct approach; the second by using an indirect approach.

The direct approach would follow on the heels of your opening statement above, perhaps in the following form:

'Since I have indicated some flexibility in the matter of compensation, I would be glad to hear from you the salary figure you have in mind for this post.'

The indirect approach is based on the fact that most executive compensation schemes today are indeed a 'package'. Salary is one major part of that package. However, perks, with their tax advantages, can make an important contribution to your real, bottom-line income.

Using this fact as your point of entry in responding, you have every reason to pose the following question.

'Since salary is directly taxable, I would be glad if we could discuss your compensation scheme as a totality. To pick one non-salary item at random, does your company have a share option plan for its executives?'

Depending on how the other person answers this question, you are in a position to pursue the subject as might be appropriate. If, for example, your interviewer's answer deals only with share options, you should be prepared to move the subject along with your next specific question. This could be: 'Does the package include life insurance paid for by the company?'

These are only two of the points to check out. Others include:

- a major medical plan;
- retirement provisions;
- use of a car;
- reimbursement of expenses;
- executive dining privileges.

You will notice that holiday time is not included in this list for reasons that I hope are apparent.

What have we accomplished by this excursion into non-salary items? First, if the fringe benefits are attractive, this is important information for you to have in relation to your discussion of salary. Secondly, if the benefits are not generous, the other party may feel their bargaining position to be weakened, perhaps inducing them to compensate by treating the matter of salary in a more generous way.

But, the third and biggest advantage is that you have separated the interviewer from their original question ('How much are you asking?') by a period of several minutes. This allows you to reverse the question. Immediately after you have ticked off in your mind the last question concerning benefits, you can follow through with this one.

'Thank you for this information which I find very interesting. Now I am curious to know what salary figure goes with the package.'

This switch might not work of course. The interviewer may give you a peculiar look, saying in effect: 'What's going on here? That was the question *I* put to you and I'm still waiting for the answer.'

However, you have lost nothing, but you have gained needed information. More important, perhaps, is the probability that a smart interviewer will give you a high score as a negotiator – a talent they might well want to put to the service of their company or department.

If you do find yourself blocked in this fashion, your fall-back point must be well defined in order to avoid any continued appearance of being evasive. At the same time, you should continue to side-step the trap of specifying an 'anticipated' or 'asking' salary. With these two thoughts in mind, try a response along the following lines:

'While I have no fixed salary requirement, you may find it helpful to know my present [or most recent] rate of compensation. It comes to £45 000 per year. Naturally I would hope to improve on this figure.'

(By way of reminder, the figure to be quoted is a combination of your yearly salary figure, plus your estimate of the value of fringe benefits capitalised on an annual basis.)

The ball is now in the court of the interviewer. It is quite possible that they will not wish to 'negotiate' in the course of a first meeting. In this case the figure may simply be noted as a point of reference should a further contact be made later on.

Another possible scenario could be that the interviewer finds your figure unrealistically high in relation to what they plan to offer. In this case, the reply might be:

'I'm afraid we have a problem. You understand, of course, that we have a salary policy to preserve a balance between people of similar responsibilities. I'm sorry to tell you that we could not visualise paying even the amount that you are earning. In view of this fact, I must ask you if you wish to continue being considered as a candidate.'

Your reply to this question will depend largely, of course, on your degree of interest in the post, the sector of activity and the company itself. If your feelings are positive on these points, you can keep the ball in play without marking yourself down, as you would do by saying: 'Well, OK, I might consider taking a pay cut.' Such a reply cheapens you in the eyes of your interviewer. It gives the impression that you have few or no other possibilities and hints that you may be acting from desperation.

You can keep the door open and at the same time avoid such negative vibrations by phrasing your response in a different, more proactive fashion:

'Naturally, I am somewhat disappointed to learn that there is a gap between our two needs. One reason is that I am genuinely interested

in the post we are discussing and I also like what I have heard about your organisation. By nature, I am not averse to making an investment in my own future and I'd like to know something about the growth possibilities. For example, would a salary review within – say the next six months or a year – be a realistic expectation?'

If the interviewer's reply is negative, my advice is to break off the negotiation at this point. On the other hand, the interviewer in this case is probably working within a fixed budget. The possibility exists that an upgrading of salary could take place at the time of the next budgetary period. Furthermore, a merit raise, based on good performance, is far easier for a manager to justify than the hiring of an outsider at a salary that is out of line with the rate of pay for existing staff.

Obviously there will be technical questions that you will want to pose, based on your type of activity. At the same time your interviewer may often have a few surprises in store for you. Here I refer to the unorthodox, unexpected questions that are bound to pop up from time to time. In the next chapter we will examine some of these from my own case-book.

CHAPTER 10

Unorthodox questions

Many – perhaps most – interviewers have pet questions of which they are very fond. While it is impossible to predict the nature of many of these, experience suggests that you will be able to turn any of them to your advantage if you maintain a proactive attitude. Here are some examples of pet questions.

QUESTION 1

THE QUESTION (at the very start of your meeting): '*Since this is simply a get-acquainted meeting, let me turn the agenda over to you. You might start my telling me about yourself – or I can tell you something about our organisation. Which would you prefer?*'

A REACTIVE RESPONSE: '*I am an experienced research manager in the field of animals foods ...*'

A PROACTIVE RESPONSE: '*I'd be glad to have any information you'd care to give me about the position you are seeking to fill, as well as about your company's operations.*'

Interviewers who use this opening gambit have a fixed idea as to the response they are looking for. If you reply by talking about yourself you may, with luck, look forward to a 20-minute meeting. Even this 20 minutes is motivated by elementary ideas of courtesy on the part of the host. In truth, the interviewer's mind has been made up; the candidate simply does not understand the rudiments of negotiation, is not a listener and probably has problems in conducting human relations. All of this may or may not be accurate. It makes no difference. A pet question is usually dear to the questioner's heart. It provides them with an easy way to screen out candidates and to economise with their time.

QUESTION 2

THE QUESTION: *'We have talked at some length about your job history, Mr Smith. Now let's take a moment to help me understand you as a person. I'd be interested to know, for example, what you consider to be your greatest single strength as a human being.'*

A REACTIVE RESPONSE (after some hesitation): *'That's a hard question to answer, but I consider myself to be a person of honesty and integrity. I also am a very hard worker.'*

INTERVIEWER: *'The question had to do with one single quality.'*

CANDIDATE: *'Oh, yes, of course. In that case, integrity.'*

Please don't think I am opposed to honesty and integrity. What the reactive response fails to take into account is that the world, fortunately, abounds in honest people. The same statement applies to people who work hard. These are qualities that the interviewer is ready to assume, with reason or otherwise, will be displayed by the majority of executives.

A PROACTIVE RESPONSE: *'While it is not easy to select one single quality, I feel that my ability to organise groups of people into an efficient working unit may well be my strongest point.'*

This is an acceptable response if the need of the company is indeed related to problems of organisation. The strength you select should be chosen according to some function you are expected to perform. Need I also add that the quality you wish to highlight must really exist. Faking your response would be even less desirable than offering a reactive answer. However, we all possess a variety of strengths and you are perfectly free to choose any one among four or five that seem to you to be outstanding.

Your reply, whatever it may be, permits the interviewer to move on to the second part of the scenario.

QUESTION 3

THE QUESTION: *'Of course organisational skills are always useful. But let's for a moment look at the other side of the coin. What do you judge to be your single greatest weakness?'*

A REACTIVE RESPONSE: *'Well, people sometimes accuse me of being overly concerned with details.'*

I have deliberately chosen one of the most damaging qualities that a candidate can expose, except in the unlikely case that the vacant position deals with very small fragments of some staff assignment. The candidate is nearly always addressing a manager of some sort – very probably a mover and shaker by nature. Executives who get lost in detail are almost bound to be anathema to him. There are other, almost equally damaging, answers to the question. How to avoid them is best seen in the light of the more productive reply, as follows.

A PROACTIVE RESPONSE: *'Because I like to see tangible results from my efforts, I am afraid I tend to be irritated by any kind of slowing down. At such times there is no doubt my irritation sometimes shows and rubs some people up the wrong way. Do you feel this represents a serious weakness in the job we are talking about?'*

I repeat, the response must be rooted in reality. It also will relate ideally to the profile of the position under discussion. We all know that there are certain qualities that represent both weaknesses and strengths at the same time. In the case of the proactive example above, you are speaking of a quality shared by many, indeed the majority, of line managers. In short, you are taking the opportunity to confirm that there is a meeting of minds between you and the other person.

QUESTION 4

THE QUESTION: *'In looking back over your career to date, can you recall any situations where you were involved in interpersonal conflicts? If so, I'd be interested in hearing an example.'*

A REACTIVE RESPONSE: *'No, I have always got along well with all my colleagues.'*

There are two dangers with this kind of reply. First, 'getting along well' with people, or any similar description, smacks of a bland personality whose chief motivation is to avoid any form of confrontation. Secondly, the statement, even if it is true, is hardly believable.

A PROACTIVE RESPONSE: *'Of course I have been in some situations of conflict. During one difficult period, for example, I had to fire several people. On that occasion, and I believe in any others, I feel I have always acted in the best interests of my organisation. Do you feel it is possible for managers to be able to avoid a certain amount of conflict?'*

QUESTION 5

THE QUESTION: *'If we wish to contact you, may we phone you at your office?'*

A REACTIVE RESPONSE: *'Yes, that would be OK.'*

If you are presently employed, this answer can be damaging. It implies that your employer is informed of, or may even have motivated, your search elsewhere. It looks like you are either being pushed out of your job or that your company feels no pain at the prospect of your departure.

A PROACTIVE RESPONSE: *'I am sorry, but that might compromise my situation. Either I could arrange to telephone you at a date you suggest or you could leave a message at my home number where I have a telephone-answering machine. Which would be more convenient?'*

QUESTION 6

THE QUESTION: *'Can you supply me with three or four business references?'*

A REACTIVE RESPONSE: *'Yes, of course.'*

Our discussion here is still focused on the first meeting with a possible employer. It is premature to provide names and addresses at this time for two reasons. First you are setting up a situation where later on you may find yourself giving the same names over and over again. This is particularly true if you are, as I hope, conducting a widespread search to identify all the potential job positions that might be available to you. Your referees will probably be amenable to replying to the first one or two requests. After that, there is every possibility that they will become increasingly annoyed. The second reason why you should delay giving out such names concerns your present employer, if you are still in a job. If you give out names of people within your company you are indicating that your departure is 'by common consent'.

A PROACTIVE RESPONSE: *'Of course I will give you as many references as you wish. However, you will understand that I prefer not to trouble my contacts with repeated requests. Would you be agreeable to postponing this matter until our exploration together is further advanced?'*

QUESTION 7

THE QUESTION: *'Here is a sheet of paper. While we are together, I would like to have a specimen of your handwriting. Please write down a few sentences on any subject you wish.'*

A REACTIVE RESPONSE: *To start writing.*

Graphology is sometimes used as a supplementary means of screening candidates. There is no point in trying to evade a request for a handwriting specimen. However, to produce a sample from the uncomfortable side of the desk and at the same time to do so under scrutiny could influence your writing style in a negative way. It is best to make an effort to avoid this possible handicap.

A PROACTIVE RESPONSE: *'I'd be glad to give you a specimen of my writing. Would it be possible for me to do this at home? That way you will have a more representative sample.'*

The interviewer may insist. In this case, yield gracefully. The thought you have expressed is valid and you lose nothing by making an entirely proper suggestion.

QUESTION 8

THE QUESTION: *'I'm afraid that we must deal with the matter of your age. You are 47. The president of our company is only 42 and our normal practice is to hire people just out of university. Despite your excellent record, the age difference poses a problem.*

A REACTIVE ANSWER: *'Yes, I am 47, but my health is just as good and my energy level is just as high as it was when I was 30.'*

A PROACTIVE ANSWER: *'I can well understand the problem. None the less, at my age a person has been exposed to a wide variety of problems and solutions. One way to make these values available to you would be to arrange a contract of limited duration. This would have the merit of setting the minds of your colleagues at ease. At the same time I believe I can make an important enough contribution to cause the company to consider a more permanent arrangement at the end of a year. If not, a younger person who has benefitted from my experience would take over my post. Would such an arrangement make sense to you?'*

In this response you are presenting management with an attractive offer since they obviously do not have the experience they seek within their own team. At the same time, you will have to recognise that such a trade-off puts you in a position of some vulnerability. One year in office does not give you much time to win loyalty and to show results, particularly if you have young lions under or around you who are eager and ready to take over. Thus this response is a fall-back position to be used only in three cases:

1. *if you must leave your present company;*

2. *if you are without a job; or*

3. *if you are sure that age is such an insuperable block as to make your chances impossible under a normal hiring procedure.*

QUESTION 9

THE QUESTION (to a woman): *'The position requires a certain amount of travel and so probably is more naturally suited to a man. I would be interested, for this reason, to know if you intend to marry and to have (more) children?'*

A REACTIVE RESPONSE: *'At the present time I can say positively that I have no such intentions.'*

This answer of course is a non-answer and will be perceived as such. Your plans and intentions could be subject to change the following morning.

A PROACTIVE RESPONSE: *'I made up my mind a long time ago to be a professional person. At the same time I do not rule out the possibility of having (more) children. Rather than be in a position of doing a mediocre job as a mother and as a business woman, I have already decided to hire a full-time nanny to care for the baby if the situation arises. However, let me assure you that I presently have no plans for new arrivals.'*

CHAPTER 11

Winding it up

Just as the start of your meeting is of prime importance, so is the way in which you wind it up.

If your interviewer is polite, you will be given non-verbal signals that the time is running out. Frequent glances at the clock, not pursuing new subjects as they arise and a certain amount of shuffling of papers may be among these signals. Pay attention to them and begin to plan an orderly retreat. An interviewer under increasing pressure of time will almost certainly feel a growing irritation, particularly if the situation is exacerbated by you ignoring the signals.

Possibly the interviewer has lost track of the passage of time breaks off abruptly, saying, 'I am sorry but I realise I have a meeting that begins at 11 o'clock. Thank you for your visit. You can be assured that we'll be in touch with you as to the possibility of a further contact.'

THE REACTIVE RESPONSE: *'Thank you, I've enjoyed our meeting very much. The position we've discussed really appeals to me and I'll be looking forward to hearing further from you.'*

What's wrong with this reply? First of all, the fact that the job attracts *you* is not an element of prime importance to the other person. It is quite natural that the interviewer's concern is what you can do for them and their company. More important, you are leaving open a situation that could prove irksome for you in the future. You do not know when to expect a follow-through or even if you will hear from the interviewer again. After your meeting the days and weeks may go by to a point where you are no longer sure whether you are dealing with a live possibility or one without even a hope of any result. Finally, you will consider contacting the interviewer on your own initiative. This step will almost certainly either be taken too late or – without you having knowledge of the timing – too early, before they are ready to give you any definite information. In either case you are likely to find yourself dealing with a secretary since such follow-up calls, if uninvited, are among the most susceptible to screening.

A consequence of this lack of information arises when you have one or more other negotiations pending. Let's say that the situation described above happens to be the post that interests you the most. However, a second possibility has progressed to a final stage. It is not the ideal job, but meets most of your requirements. If you reach the point of being pressed for a decision on the second possibility, you will want to have the information you lack concerning the first possibility. What precisely are your chances of getting the job?

If you are fortunate enough to have several serious negotiations under way at the same time, the matter of dates for decisions – even if they are necessarily approximate – becomes one of prime importance.

A PROACTIVE RESPONSE (PART 1): *'About when do you think you will have completed your first screening of candidates?'*

INTERVIEWER: *'I should think we'd need about three weeks to reach that point.'*

A PROACTIVE RESPONSE (PART 2):*'I'm afraid we may have a problem of timing here. As you may imagine I am talking to a number of people located in and out of town, and I expect to be doing a considerable amount of travelling during the weeks ahead. I am very interested in what I've heard today and both of us might be in a position of some frustration if you are unable to make contact. To make sure this doesn't happen, may I suggest that I telephone you three weeks from today?'*

INTERVIEWER: *'OK. Let's plan it that way.'*

Or, or course, the interviewer may not agree, saying: 'Thanks for the suggestion, but I'm sure we'll find a way to catch up with you.'

Even if you receive this rather unlikely response, you will still have won the important point of having an approximate deadline. There is nothing to prevent you from phoning in, say, four weeks, in an effort to learn how matters stand, by saying to the secretary on the phone: 'I understood from Mrs Jones that a decision was due to be made around this time and I would like to speak to her about it.' In this way you can at least offer a specific statement tracing back to the boss.

In making your departure from the meeting you will want to keep in mind two essential points.

1 Do not forget to address a genial farewell to the secretary and receptionist. Obvious perhaps? Yes, but ... The 'but' is added because of a common tendency to become so involved in flash-backs of your meeting that it is easy to leave in a state of self-

absorption. Remember that many executives make it a practice to check the impressions of their aides in the outer office. They know that a candidate can present an entirely different face to people who are lower in the pecking order than the face they show to the interviewer. Was the candidate nervous, impatient or depressed? These can be subjects of interest that are supplementary to the meeting itself. Keep in mind that many secretary/boss relationships can be very close indeed.

2 It is not unknown for the interviewer to accompany the candidate to the door or lift while continuing to chat. These few minutes can take on a deceptively relaxed character. The rule to follow here is: 'The meeting is not over until you have left the building.' I can cite examples where the impression left behind by a candidate was seriously tarnished by a sudden spasm of spontaneity – simply due to a relief of tension.

THE FOLLOW-UP LETTER

Surprisingly few candidates send a letter of acknowledgement after a first meeting. No doubt they feel this to be a meaningless formality, but it can be a good idea. It is one more form of making contact, causing the interviewer to recall you and your situation. Since most jobs are filled after meetings with a considerable number of candidates, it is easy for any one of them – yourself included – to become lost in the memory of a parade of faces and career histories. Whatever steps you can take to ensure that you don't fade from the interviewer's memory are useful.

One way to add force to your letter is to make it a businesslike document. A typical letter might read as follows.

Dear Mr Smith
This confirms our telephone conversation yesterday afternoon in which I stated I would be free to commence a new position in 60 days.

I found our meeting stimulating and wish to thank you for the details you gave me concerning the position you are seeking to fill. I have very positive feelings about the post and your company, and want you to know of my willingness to pursue our discussions.

As we agreed, I'll plan to telephone on 15 September to discuss the possibility of a second meeting.

Yours sincerely
Thomas Jones

CHAPTER 12

The second and third meetings

The executive job seeker is rarely offered a position at the close of an initial meeting. If this is the case, you should ask yourself why a company should be acting in haste and without serious reflection. Among the several thousand situations of change with which I have been in contact, I can recall only one instance where a successful change resulted from an offer made at the first contact.

The situations you might meet in the second and third contacts with the same organisations are subject to too many variations to provide a scenario that might be realistic. One type of call-back might be for you to meet an executive at a higher level than the person you originally met. A variation of this is a situation in which you are introduced to several key members of the management team. On other occasions a feature of such follow-through appointments is a tour of the facilities, during which you may be making contact with possible future subordinates and peers.

Regardless of the exact format of such meetings, certain features are likely to stand out. For example, with each successive contact, the number of candidates for a position becomes smaller. Very likely the emphasis will be less on your experience and specialised knowledge than on the quality of your human contact. How well will you 'fit in'?

Beyond doubt there will be more precision on the question of salary, fringe benefits and working conditions. In this connection, the negotiating techniques I recommend in Chapter 19 continue to be useful. You and your future employer have already established that your respective needs in the matter of compensation are in general reciprocal. The time has now come for a clear understanding of this important point.

No matter how satisfactory verbal agreements may appear to be, you are well advised never to consider an employment agreement final on either side until there has been an exchange of letters summarising all points of understanding signed by both employer and employee.

I can bring to mind several situations, one of them particularly dramatic, where an executive was convinced all arrangements had been finalised, only to learn with a sense of shock that this was not the case. The outstanding example was a laboratory manager for a major manufacturer of soaps and other household products. Blocked in his progression he sought – and thought he had found – a similar but far more important role with a world-renowned company in the same field. He shook hands to conclude the arrangement and, because of the reputation of his 'future employer', had no hesitation in handing in his notice to his current management. After having made arrangements to move his family to the new location, he received the following telegram:

Regret restructuration of our research department forces abandonment of the plan to utilise your services. Letter follows.

A letter containing amplified regrets arrived swiftly. It changed nothing. A highly specialised laboratory director found himself unemployed, demoralised and confronted with a particularly tough job search.

Every person has the right to accept a position contingent on receipt of a letter of employment recapitulating all major conditions agreed upon. Beware of the company that takes the following line: 'In our outfit we do not need written agreements. It is a sign of our team's spirit and mutual goodwill that we all accept each other's word. . . .' This is an elementary form of manipulation that simply opens the door to misunderstanding and mistrust. In the event of any later disagreement on terms, it is not hard to imagine whose recollection is the most likely to prevail.

ESSENTIALS TO BE COVERED IN THE LETTER OF AGREEMENT

The following is a check-list of matters on which you should reach a firm verbal agreement, with each point confirmed in writing.

1 The date of commencement of employment.

2 Remuneration.

3 Fringe benefits (if applicable):
  (a)   retirement plan;
  (b)   car type and conditions of use;
  (c)   stock options;

(d) life insurance;

(e) executive dining room privileges.

4 Method of compensating for travel and other expenses.

5 Notice of termination of employment required from either party.

6 Holiday period and how computed.

7 Other terms as may be covered on the company's manual of personnel procedures and practices.

8 Coverage of relocation costs of moving overseas (if applicable):
    (a) housing allowance;
    (b) how travelling and other business expenses are to be reimbursed;
    (c) schooling allowance for children;
    (d) currency in which salary is to be computed and rate at which payments in local currency are to be computed in terms of home currency;
    (e) provision for annual visit to homeland for self and family;
    (f) provision for medical expenses;
    (g) guarantee of employment in homeland at end of tour of duty overseas;
    (h) provision for income tax equalisation.

GET FULLY INFORMED

Many presidents and managing directors are excellent salespeople. This ability is usually a requirement of their job. The job seeker is, however, the major risk taker in accepting a new position. It is vital for the job seeker, even more than for the employer, to make certain that any future commitment is made under conditions that offer the best possible chance of a successful outcome.

For this reason, namely the minimisation of risk, you are well advised to seek the fullest possible information about the company you are contemplating joining. I have seen too many cases of sad – and rude – awakenings not to add these words of advice. Take the situation of a high-level applications engineer in the chemical field, who joined a small company whose income figures had been increasing 50 per cent each year for five years. This future seemed unlimited – until he entered the company and learned that the impressive sales increases were being scored by the simple expedient of selling the company's products at below real cost. Two months after he began work, his management was forced to seek the protection of the courts.

Between the frequent existence of a 'trial period' and the difficulty of obtaining factual financial information, the risks faced by the new arrival are considerable. In the case of a larger, publicly owned company, facts and figure are relatively easy to obtain. However, smaller private companies abound. In such situations, there are several ways of obtaining the information you need before signing your employment agreement.

- You may be able to trace a friend or colleague who is with a company operating in the same field of activity as your prospective employer. It is not unusual for companies to be in possession of excellent information about the competition (and a certain degree of chauvinism on the part of your contact may have to be taken into account).

- Talk to your bank manager. While they may not be able, for reasons of ethical practice, to give you precise figures, you will be able to interpret with some precision their attitude towards the subject of your enquiry. After all, your bank manager has a real interest in your own future financial well-being.

- Various credit-rating sources will supply, for a reasonable fee, their evaluation of a company.

To summarise, we should recognise that it is flattering to have what appears to be an excellent job offer. It is also a relief to be able to bring to an end a diligent, difficult search for the right post. Yet, at the same time, you have made an important investment in your career to date. A few additional hours spent in researching the realistic outlook of your future will be a small price to pay to ensure the protection and future growth of that investment.

CHAPTER 13
The advice visit

Up to this point, our discussion has focused on the exchanges that are likely to occur in the course of a classical job interview.

Obviously, not all first contacts with potential employers are of this nature; few of us, for example, are so short of friends and contacts that we can't find one or more people with whom we can talk about future possibilities. In fact, some seekers of change are even too well supplied with such potential targets. Take the example of the 47-year-old assistant managing director of a large manufacturer of equipment for the textile industry. With the onset of the recession, his company was forced to cut back and his job was eliminated. After 18 years of devotion to his employer and to his job, he found himself almost literally in a state of shock. As he learned to live with his new situation, however, he felt himself able to see the matter in clearer perspective. Or so he thought. 'After all,' he told himself, 'think of all the people I've known and had good relations with. Surely one or more of these will help me find a good job.'

As with many others in a similar position, my friend began a series of 'contacts' stretching out over a period of three months: lunch with one person; drinks with another; visits to the offices of people to whom he was referred by his original contacts. At the end of the three months of activity, he awaited the results he was sure would be forthcoming. Unfortunately, there were none. In all, he lost five months of valuable time – valuable since time in a period without income represents a direct and important financial loss. Even more serious, my friend, like others whose hopes have been raised, found himself the victim of a second rude awakening. Not only had he lost his job due to no fault of his own, but now he had the feeling of being let down and undervalued by people who were in a position to appreciate his qualities and the quality of his work. To feelings of injustice were added feelings of bitterness. Such an emotional mix is not designed to enhance one's performance in later contacts with prospective employers.

An executive who was more sophisticated in job hunting would not be so affected by such a negative result from approaches to personal contacts. Such a person would understand that the difficulties arise from the very nature of this particular method of exploration and would not be blind to the fact that few company owners or managers are inclined to bring friends into their organisations. Such executives know that the quality of a hierarchical relation and a friendly relation are entirely different, and that a mixture of the two can spell damage to both.

What, then, of the contact with a third person, an introduction which has been arranged by a friend? Here, too, lurks an evident problem. Put quite simply, the third party is agreeing to meet the job seeker primarily to please the person who made the introduction. This contact is likely to ask for copies of the visitor's CV, promising to show it to several people. The job hunter leaves the office filled with good feelings and real hope of a future breakthrough. When this is not forthcoming, the job hunter may wake up to the fact that the motivation behind the meeting was wrong from the start. The interest and the friendliness of the other person was not towards the stranger across the desk, but towards the friend who was the instigator of the meeting.

THE ADVICE VISIT

With these points in mind let us examine the merits of another type of meeting which in my experience is far more likely to lead to a positive outcome. I call this type of contact the 'advice visit'. The model advice visit has three main characteristics:

1 the visit should be made to a person you do not know but who is on a general management level;
2 the kind of business with which the person is associated must be one with which you do not have direct familiarity; and, most important
3 the visit must not in any way be made with the intention, or even the vague hope, of receiving a job offer.

Each of these points requires explanation.

In the first place, we should assume that, as is usually the case, you possess certain skills which are transferable from one type of enterprise to another; such areas of expertise fall under various broad headings as finance, sales, engineering or plant management; at the same time your use of your skills has been confined to one, two or possibly three different kinds of business settings. Now that the time has come for you to change jobs – whether as a result of choice or necessity – you are faced with the need to explore as widely as possible the opportunities available to you. In undertaking such research, there is no law, rule or regulation that dictates a need for you to confine your research to sectors of activity in which you have first-hand experience. At such a time of change, remarkably few people think in terms of exploring the kinds of business in which they have a natural interest, perhaps simply by predilection or, more tangibly, because of a hobby or other interest outside their day-to-day job. One reason for such limited horizons, I suspect, is that we do not know, from a practical point of view, whether our particular experience with a given product or service has any real pragmatic application in a different kind of business with which we have very little practical acquaintance.

Here we have the basic premise of the advice visit. It is a meeting, not to 'ask for a job', but rather to have the facts as to the practicability of conducting a job search within a particular branch of business or the professions. It is one thing to pose such a question to a career counsellor or a recruiter – both of whom are by necessity in possession of second-hand, sometimes out-of-date, knowledge. It is quite another matter to get the answer from people who are well placed within a given sector.

Why do I recommend that this kind of visit be arranged with directors you do not know either directly or through a mutual acquaintance? The answer is very simple. A person who agrees to see you as a result of a direct 'cold' contact is motivated only by their willingness to meet you. This person has not said 'yes' for the wrong reasons – out of personal consideration for you or courtesy to a mutual friend.

The advice visit cannot be faked. Your interest in the other person's kind of business must be genuine. If it is, the results of such meetings can be as stimulating as they are unexpected.

I am thinking of one client who was managing director of a small food-processing business owned by his family. A 'policy difference' with his father clearly suggested that he should look elsewhere. Of course, the food industry remained within his target area, but he was restless and thought in terms of a change of industry. This man had a number of outside interests, but everything to do with sailing and boats stood out from the rest. He decided to explore the possibilities of using his professional abilities within a nautical setting. The decision triggered off a variety of advice visits to marine architects, to boat builders and to celebrated yachtspeople. To each, the question was the same: 'Is there a place within the industry for a person possessing my particular combination of educational background [he held an MBA from Harvard], business experience [finance and management] and interests [notably sailboat racing]. 'Piece by piece the information he sought accumulated. Based on these facts he discerned a gap in the range of small sailboats then being offered to the public. Among other characteristics such as speed, the boat he envisaged would be light enough to be towed to the sea without effort by a car, yet sturdy enough to survive in any sea conditions. My client then returned to one of the architects he had first contacted. Together they produced a sketch of the craft he imagined. A boat builder expressed interest and several parties teamed up to produce a prototype. Ultimately a major boat builder bought the licence to construct and market the boat.

After an outstanding success at the annual French boat show, the vessel is currently being constructed and widely sold in the US and other countries. My client today finds himself in charge of a company exploiting the rights to the manufacture of the first boat, while actively producing new designs and prototypes. With the capital he has amassed, he now plans to add a production facility to his design and exploitation activities.

Similar examples abound of executives who have succeeded in combining pleasure and work in positions that offer them the maximum of job satisfaction.

'But how', people frequently ask, 'can a stranger walk into the office of a managing director simply for the purpose of asking questions that, in essence, are self-serving?'

The answer is that the difficulty is more apparent than real. To understand why this is so, we must analyse the motivations that can prompt a busy individual to give up some time for such a meeting. There could be at least three positive motivations:

- people absorbed in their work enjoy talking about it to those rare individuals who are genuinely interested.
- everyone enjoys the role of authority and the advice visit places the other person uncontestably in this position;
- most people take some pleasure in giving a hand to their fellows – particularly if their contribution neither costs money nor makes an important demand on their time.

The traditional 'job interview' tends to be a meeting involving some degree of tension, more often than not ending with a rejection of one party by the other. Because of these aspects, such meetings can hardly be undertaken as a potential source of pleasure to either party. This is one reason why many executives seeking a change find it difficult to arrange meetings in the role of job candidate. Earlier we discussed the use of transactional analysis in the conduct of pre-employment meetings. We saw that the objective was to ensure, insofar as possible, that the conversation was based on an Adult–Adult relationship.

The advice visit is entirely different in its nature. The transaction is quite deliberately undertaken as a Parent–Child encounter. On the one side, we have a person (yourself) who makes no claims whatsoever to knowledge that the other person (the host) manifestly possesses. For this reason, the person receiving you will be thoroughly at ease in their position as authority. You, too, need to feel no tension since, despite your professed ignorance, you have absolutely nothing to lose and much to gain from your contact. In short, the stage is set for a pleasurable exchange.

The moment has now come to explore with some care the objectives to be accomplished in the course of a typical advice visit. Is the purpose solely to collect information to help you in your exploration of possible job opportunities?

Of course, this is one important aspect of the meeting. In addition, however, you can benefit from two valuable by-products. First, you are in the process of gaining valuable experience in talking about yourself in an objective fashion. In this connection, you will recall the stress I placed on the importance of asking questions during pre-employment meetings. The advice visit is, of course, squarely based on a questioning technique and therefore is helpful in establishing the right patterns for 'job interviews'. A second way you can profit from the advice visit is to obtain referrals at the end of your meeting on to other key executives; thus widening your spectrum of contacts.

How to arrange advice visits

Depending on your particular skills as a communicator, you may choose to make your first contact either by letter or by telephone. If by letter, each word must be carefully chosen to convey the message outlined below. If by telephone, you should be in possession of some ability to deal effectively with the executive's guardian angel – the secretary.

In either case, your most effective approach will take the following form.

1 You are simply asking for a few minutes of the time of the other person.

2 Why? Because you are contemplating a career change and this person is in possession of the answers to certain questions which will be helpful to you in charting your future course.

3 You have a profound interest in the field of activity the person's enterprise occupies, but you are in no sense putting yourself forward for a post.

4 Your letter should, of course, include a very brief introduction of yourself, concentrating on your present activities.

5 Should you make contact by letter, state that you will telephone in one week with a view to establishing a convenient time and date to meet.

If your approach is well handled, you will succeed in arranging meetings with 50 per cent of your original contacts.

A typical advice visit

When you find yourself face to face with the executive you wished to meet, keep in mind that some time probably has elapsed since you first suggested the meeting. Your host may have forgotten the original reason for the meeting, if indeed they were ever entirely clear on this point. As a result, the host will often open the conversation in a questioning or even sceptical way:

'I'm glad to see you, Mr Smith, but I must confess I am not quite sure about the precise reason you asked for this meeting.'

SMITH: *'I hope I made it clear when I contacted you that my purpose is not in any way to ask you for a job or to try to sell you anything. None the less, my visit does have to do with my future career direction. I have long been fascinated by the very human aspects of the hotel business and have thought of including this kind of activity among my possible targets in my future job exploration. Naturally, I would like to avoid wasting my own time and that of other people if my background bears no relation to posts that might be available. A person in your position has a view on the entire range of activities in hotel management, so I am here to pose the question: "Do my experience and background have any real value within the framework of your business?"'*

THE HOST: *'You understand that I have very little information about you to help me answer your question. Perhaps you have brought your CV to give me a clearer picture.'*

SMITH: *'As you know I am in the process of examining the realistic possibilities for the future. I thought it best to create my CV on the results of my research. However, I can give you the main elements of my experience verbally.'*

(At this point Smith devotes three to five minutes outlining his background and areas of competence. This 'potted history' should be well prepared and well organised in advance to avoid wasting any time. Above all, any such listing of your experiences should start with the present situation and work backwards in time.)

THE HOST: *'You seem to have a good professional background. I confess I find it hard to understand why you wish to leave the commodity business to risk a change to a field so completely different as the hotel business.'*

SMITH: *'I'm not surprised that you might wonder about the wisdom of such a move. The answer becomes clearer when you realise how little contact with people I have [had] in my present [or last] job. I like working with others, both inside and outside my organisation, and I would very much miss this aspect of my activities.'*

The host will perhaps have other questions before giving any advice. When they do, it is likely to take one of two forms.

Alternative 1

THE HOST: *'I think I can understand your urge to make a change and I accept the fact that you are good with figures. None the less, I'd advise you to look somewhere else than in the hotel field. Except in rare cases, we have all been through hotel school and the few exceptions to this rule just don't correspond to your experience.'*

SMITH (replying to Alternative 1): *'Naturally, I'm a bit disappointed to have to eliminate hotels as a possibility. However, since we are together, I'd like to ask you to put yourself in my position. Based on the information you now have about me, do you have any suggestions as to other kinds of activity that in your view might be more suitable?'*

THE HOST: *'Well, there is one possibility you might try. The transportation field could well give you the people contact you seek, while making some use of your commodity experience.'*

SMITH: *'That sounds like an excellent idea! Tell me, do you know of someone well placed in airlines or shipping whom I might contact in order to have the same kind of talk that we have had today?'*

(Note: It is important that you use similar phrasing in order to avoid any suggestion that you might use your host's name as a reference to help you obtain a job. Any such indication might defeat the objective which is to establish a chain of ongoing contacts.)

Alternative 2

THE HOST: *'I feel your idea to enter the hotel field is, on the whole, realistic. You are evidently a good person with figures and at the same time can make good contact with people. Both qualities are important in our work. Yes, I think you might well give it a try.'*

SMITH: *'Thank you. That is good news. As I told you, I will soon be preparing a CV incorporating what I have learned from you and others. Would you like me to send you a copy for your own possible interest?'*

(Note: The reference in this reply to what you have learned from 'him and others' conveys the fact that your researches have extended beyond your host's office. It is evident that the impression that you have made is a good one and that you have the ability to make a contribution to his kind of business. The possibility that you might ultimately be engaged by one of his competitors could be one incentive for him to give serious thought to your candidature.)

Obviously the foregoing scenario is simply a typical model of an advice visit. Within such a framework there can be wide variations, depending on your particular situation. However, the basic theme emerges clearly from this one example.

1 The advice call is best made to a person you do not know either at first hand or through a mutual contact.

2 The request is simply for a few minutes of a person's time.

3 You must make it abundantly clear that you are not hoping to be offered a job and this must be subjectively eliminated from your possible motivations.

4 Your interest in the other person's type of business must be genuine. Obviously, the advice visit makes no sense if the sector of activity you want to explore is similar to settings in which you already have some experience and knowledge.

5 Your objectives are:
   (a)   to base your future research on a solid foundation of current information;
   (b)   to practise, without the possibility of missing out on a specific job, your manner of presenting yourself;
   (c)   to have the possibility of receiving suggestions as to other sec tors for exploration that you may, as a prisoner of your own

particular experience, not have thought of;

(d)   to be referred on to other persons in order to enlarge your chain of contacts.

You may well find reasons for making similar contacts other than to ask advice concerning a type of business. One such exchange might be based on a contemplated move to a new city, county or country about which you seek information on local working and living conditions. Once again, you are regarding the other person as an authority who can help you fill a gap in your knowledge.

In summary, a typical 'job interview' is a meeting that implies a certain tension, while the advice visit is by nature a relaxed, open communication with the possibility of unexpected, and frequently exciting, new career vistas.

CHAPTER 14

Putting it together

Our discussion up to this point has put forward a great many suggestions, from the start of your goal setting through to the follow-up of your negotiations for a new job or a better one inside your company.

For your quick reference there follows a check-list of critical points to which you should give careful consideration as you embark on an exploration of your next career change. Make sure that you are well prepared for your search in each of the following essential respects.

Do you have your objectives clearly in mind?

If your answer is negative, you will not know what you are negotiating *for* and this fact will leave your interviewer with the uneasy sense that they are dealing with a person who does not know their own mind – hardly a recommendation for an executive post. The time you spend sorting out your real aims and objectives is not only time well spent, but time you cannot afford to waste in other seemingly more active and specific directions. Put first things first. Goal setting is the indispensable basis for your search.

Have you checked out the messages you are sending through non-verbal communication?

This requires humility. It assumes that you are willing to ask others how you come across – even though you might receive frank answers that may jolt your own image of yourself. None the less, we have already stressed the importance of first impressions, of the fact that people hire people, not pieces of paper. If you can accept the fact that at least 50 per cent of all communication is non-verbal you will readily see the importance of your very first seconds and minutes of every meeting.

Do you understand the basic principles of transactional analysis?

If not, you may have trouble grasping the fact that falling into a 'Parent–Child' transaction can be a major block to your success in meetings that are important to your advancement. In this case, I recommend you do some reading in the subject. Basic books include *Born to Win* by James and Jongeward and *I'm OK, You're OK* by Thomas Harris. If this useful technique in human relations turns out to be a subject of more than passing interest to you, seminars are available in most Western countries. But a word of warning: before participating in such meetings, you should make sure that they are sponsored by well-known and widely accepted authorities. It is preferable to have even a superficial understanding than to become involved in groups conducted under less than professional auspices.

Are you ready to listen, to ask questions, to forgo the role of 'seller' of your services?

You have to understand the needs of the company you are addressing yourself to, just as you must define your own individual needs for job satisfaction and progression. There is no way, to my knowledge, of discovering the needs of others except by posing questions. To repeat, there is no question you will be asked in employment negotiations that cannot be answered either with a question or with a reply followed by a question. By using a questioning approach you will come to understand what the other person is looking for, and to sense the degree of 'fit' between the qualities sought and those you have to offer.

Are you prepared for a series of rejections?

You are faced with the probability that perhaps six out of seven of your first contacts with prospective employers will lead nowhere. This may be because you yourself are not enthusiastic about the enterprise or the position offered. More often, you may not have precisely the qualities that the management is seeking. This ratio of rejection is a perfectly normal fact of life in the course of a search for a new and better position. But some people are overly sensitive and interpret each non-success as a kind of failure on their part. Looking for a better job, I am convinced, is often a numbers game. If you are going to have between two and five valid job offers – and you should have this quantity in order to make a real comparison and choice between alternatives – this presupposes a large number of first contacts and, predictably, a number of dead-end meetings. It is fundamental that this perfectly classic process should not be the trigger for a downward spiral of your morale, which might damage your subsequent meetings.

Do you reach negative judgements too quickly?

Check yourself out on this point. Each first contact with a future employer should be viewed as the beginning of the game. In other words, a possibility exists and every possibility should be explored as thoroughly as possible. If you find yourself quickly turned off in a large number of first meetings – due to your impression of the person who is in front of you, because of the office decor, because, even, of such small matters as smells coming from the company cafeteria – these may be warning signals that you have a tendency to reject the other person before they might reject you.

Do you tend to place too much confidence in other people?

If so, you owe it to yourself to curb this tendency. Every change of company represents a risk. At the same time, many managing directors and company chief executives are gifted with charisma. If such prospective employers really want to engage the services of another person, they may tend to describe their company as more successful than the real facts would permit. I have seen too many cases of exploded illusions not to point out the need for acquiring every scrap of information you can about a prospective employer. What do the credit-rating services, such as Dun and Bradstreet, say about the financial stability of the enterprise? On the important question of the quality of human relations within the company, perhaps you have the means to contact a competitor to pose this question. Frequently the competition is a more objective source, strangely enough, of information than the company itself. Your own bank is another potential means of validating your information on the situation of a prospective employer.

Are you sometimes too hasty in saying 'yes'?

The same healthy scepticism suggested above is even more essential when the time comes to receive a firm offer of a job. Rule 1 is: *Never* make a commitment before you have the offer in writing. Many executives have experienced serious setbacks in their careers because they moved on the basis of a verbal promise. Such potentially damaging situations are not necessarily due to bad faith on the part of the prospective employer; sometimes situations change inside companies almost overnight. A freeze may be put in hiring. The person in charge of your activity may receive the bad news that they are being replaced. The possibility that a merger or takeover is on the horizon can change the atmosphere abruptly.

Enough said. Get it on paper and beware of situations where the management says, 'We are all one big family. We trust each other. A written commitment symbolises to us a betrayal of the kind of mutual confidence that prevails here.' Because any change is a risk you owe it to yourself and your family to take every precaution you can against making a mistake.

Once you have made a commitment do you feel 'honour-bound' to go through with the deal?

I believe most employers will agree that a candidate who has received a better offer after agreeing to join a company is well advised to choose the difficult course of breaking the prior commitment. This may create a temporary inconvenience for the company, but it is one they are equipped to cope with. On the other hand, if the candidate enters into a post feeling it is a 'duty', but knowing that the position is second-best, the organisation is taking on from the start an under-motivated executive – hardly an auspicious beginning.

For the individual, the crucial moment frequently comes when juggling two developing possibilities at once. The job seeker accepts one, fearing to lose it. Then the second materialises. If you see this kind of situation arising, be very careful how you agree to the first proposition. It is possible, for example, to agree 'in principle', subject to receiving the offer in writing. Once the letter of employment is received, it is not impossible for the candidate to identify matters that may not have been sufficiently clarified in the letter. In this case, the candidate is entitled to ask for the necessary clarification. This refinement can provide a period of time during which the second (and preferred) situation is maturing into a concrete proposition. But if this kind of delaying action is impractical, and if the most desired opportunity materialises after you have said 'yes' to another offer, face up to it, be honest and go in the direction that best seems to ensure job satisfaction and future growth.

During and after your meetings, are you seeking every possible way to get back in touch with your interviewer?

You may have been in the position of screening a number of candidates for a post yourself. If so, you are conscious of how quickly faces and names begin to blur within a few days. By finding ways to stay in contact, you are keeping your host's recollection of you, your image and your background to the fore. We have looked at ways of doing this – a phone call to clarify your date of availability or, in the course of your first meeting, to set a date to check on the possibility of a second meeting – but even after your second contact there are other possible initiatives you can take to help you stay in touch.

For example, some candidates have found it useful, if a period of non-contact is prolonged, to clip out an article in a business journal that relates to the kind of activity in which the target company is involved. A casual hand-written memo of accompaniment ('I wondered if you noticed the enclosed item that appeared in the *Gazette* yesterday. Thought this might interest you.') will suffice. Of course, any such nugget of information cannot come from the general press that your contact is likely to read regularly, so you have to look to other sources. I must add that from my personal experience I have had useful information transmitted to me in this fashion and I am always grateful to the sender for their thoughtfulness.

The essential thing to remember is not to stay out of contact for long periods of time. Another person may very well have been given the job without your even being aware of it.

Do you fish around for high-level contacts who might 'bring their influence to bear' to help you get the job?

Here I can only say that you are embarking on a potentially dangerous course. If your first contact is with the sales and marketing manager, for example, and you have a 'channel' to the executive vice-president, you may be tempted to suggest that the latter use their influence to bring about a positive result. Unfortunately, this kind of manipulation can only set off alarm bells in the mind of your original interviewer. Ask yourself, would you really feel comfortable engaging a product manager who can go over your head because of a private contact with your boss or bosses? I think the answer is sufficiently apparent not to require detailed discussion.

Do you keep complete notes on the substance of each meeting held?

In my opinion it is essential to have such a record. A few days is all it takes to begin to erase the details of each encounter from our memory bank. This is especially true if you are engaged in an active programme of contact where one meeting may easily become confused with another. At the time of the second meeting with the same enterprise you may very well find yourself groping for the essential points of your first conversation. A good clear record of what went on before is your best insurance against this kind of embarrassing communication gap.

SUMMARY

This summary of the essential points to consider in your exploration of future prospects is the framework within which you can proceed with the best possible chance of success. However, you should refer back repeatedly to the detailed points set out in the previous chapters in order, little by little, to turn the suggestions into automatic responses.

In other words, do not think of this book as merely a series of hints to be read, absorbed and then put aside. Instead, you should see it as a handbook – much as you have a handbook for your car or hi-fi equipment – in other words, a guide to be referred to repeatedly as you face new situations. The more so, since the suggestions made here do not always fit in with the habit patterns we have absorbed in the past.

Changing these patterns is not something that can occur overnight. There is no magic formula. The best you can do is to keep firmly in mind in every meeting the hallmarks of a real career position. Such a post will feature four benchmarks. In order of priority these elements will be as follows.

- *Job satisfaction.* Is it the kind of position that you are likely to be enthusiastic about when you go to work in the morning?
- *Future growth.* Does the job offer possibilities for interior growth, in the sense of learning new techniques, methods and managerial perspectives, and exterior growth, in terms of increased responsibilities and returns for your efforts?
- *The correct environment.* The word environment covers several ele-

ments. For example, can you associate with the product or service with pride and conviction? Is the geographical location to your liking? What kind of people are you likely to have around you?

- *Is your pay satisfactory?* In order of priorities, I have put salary in fourth position – not because it is unimportant but because of my conviction that you will almost inevitably realise satisfactory material rewards *if* the three previous requirements are satisfactorily met.

Part 2

THE WAY UP

Dealing with the Human Equation

CHAPTER 15

How to measure your political skills

The questions that follow are designed to help you evaluate the effectiveness of your kinetic human relations. By kinetic, I mean the kinds of contacts with people that make something happen. This definition eliminates all passive contacts for purely social reasons and even business contacts which are simply exchanges of pleasantries. Such dialogues certainly have their uses, but their chief characteristic is that very often they 'go nowhere'. In other words, it is quite possible for a person to 'like people', to 'enjoy human contact' and to 'be sociable', but at the same time to have little concept of how to produce results through the agency of other human beings.

Before addressing yourself to what follows, make sure you do not confuse this kind of passive sociability and the proactive inter-relationships that are our subject.

I am in no way discounting the possible pleasures and psychological benefits of social intercourse. Nor do I have to add, I hope, the obvious fact that pleasant day-to-day contacts have a real value in smoothing out communications between people. The important point has to do with your motivation. If at heart you are habitually seeking pleasant, trouble-free relationships as your primary goal, I can only suggest that these chapters will be of minimal value to you. However, this is probably not the case; after all, your interest in developing kinetic human relations is already demonstrated by the fact that you have read this far. In other words we can assume that you seek an effectiveness in your people contacts that will help you arrive step by step at the optimum utilisation of your abilities.

An essential starting point is to take stock of the political skills you have today. Only in this way will you be able to gauge the improvement work that needs to be done. The questions that follow may seem at first to constitute a kind of measure of naïvety versus sophistication. But this is true only to a limited extent. It is quite possible, for example, for a person to be extremely well read, to have travelled widely, to have met and overcome a multitude of challenges, and yet, in the game of office politics, to be sadly under-equipped. To profit fully from what follows, you must answer the following questions as objectively and honestly as possible.

1 Are you in frequent direct contact with your immediate boss?

Yes ☐   No ☐   More or less ☐

2 If your reply to question 1 was 'No' or 'More or less' are you persistent in your initiatives to try to establish, or improve, or re-establish communication?

Yes ☐   No ☐   More or less ☐

3 Are you careful to report to your boss information on the progress you are making towards the completion of your assignments?

Yes ☐   No ☐   Fairly ☐

4 Do you often have difficulty using people's first names, even at their initiative and invitation?

Yes ☐   No ☐

5 Do you refuse invitations to join colleagues at lunch or for a drink because 'you are too busy' or on some other pretext?

Yes ☐   No ☐   Quite often ☐

6 Do you occasionally invite colleagues to join you at lunch or for a drink?

Yes ☐   No ☐

7 If your boss finds fault with one of your staff, do you automatically, without reference to the merits of the case, rise to the defence of the person under attack?

Yes ☐   No ☐   Usually ☐

8 Between your personal and your professional life, do you create a definite line of separation, never to be crossed?

Yes ☐   No ☐

9 Even though you may already be over-burdened do you have trouble saying 'No' when additional new duties and/or responsibilities are given to you by your management without additional compensation?

Yes ☐   No ☐

10 When you are evaluating the actions of the management of your company, do you hear yourself frequently using words that imply moral judgement, such as 'justice' or 'injustice' and 'right' or 'wrong'?

Yes ☐   No ☐

11 Do you take a certain pride in your totally 'open' and 'frank' way of communicating with your management, colleagues and subordinates?

Yes ☐   No ☐   To some extent ☐

12 Do you avoid situations where office gossip is likely to be exchanged?

Yes ☐   No ☐

13 Have you ever sought and won the friendship of a person who you know has the ear of your boss?

Yes ☐   No ☐

14 Are you careful to establish and maintain a good rapport with your boss's secretary?

Yes ☐   No ☐   To some extent ☐

15 In placing your confidence in a subordinate or colleague have you sometimes later wished you had not done so?

Yes ☐   No ☐   Once or twice ☐

16 Do you resent it when management questions details of a plan or project you know you have worked out with great care?

Yes ☐   Yes, but not visibly ☐   No ☐

17 In group meetings, do others always seem to grab the floor while you are thinking through what you would like to say?

Yes ☐   No ☐   Often the case ☐

18 Does your spouse or another person close to you sometimes say that you invest too much of your time, energy and thought in the interests of your organisation without ensuring sufficient return for yourself?

Yes ☐   No ☐

19 When colleagues say they dislike office politics, do you tend to believe them?

Yes ☐   No ☐

20 Do you regard hard work, intelligence and honesty as the three golden keys to career advancement?

Yes ☐   No ☐

21 Have you ever refused, or would you now or in the future refuse, a proposed transfer to a new locality, even if acceptable by most standards?

Yes ☐   No ☐   Question not applicable ☐

22 Does your reading include non-escapist books totally outside your business or professional activities?

Yes ☐   No ☐

23 Do you tend to instinctively resist the introduction of new systems and methods that could affect the functioning of your particular area of responsibility?

Yes ☐   No ☐

24 Are you among those who 'do not suffer fools gladly' and who inwardly take some pride in the fact?

Yes ☐   No ☐

25 When there is a choice, do you tend to favour written communication over direct face-to-face discussion?

Yes ☐   No ☐

As you worked through these questions you may have reached certain conclusions about your own particular approach to human relations in an organisational context. However, the purpose of the test is not to produce conclusions but exactly the reverse. In the discussions that follow I hope instead to raise certain questions in your mind, as follows.

- *Why* did I reply as I did?
- *What* changes in my behaviour are possible and, among these, which changes are really desirable without violating deeply held convictions that are vitally important to me?
- *How* can I bring about those changes that I identify as desirable?

(If you want to check your answers to the above questions, someone talented in the art of upward mobility would reply as follows: 1 to 3, 'Yes'; 4 and 5, 'No'; 6, 'Yes'; 7 to 12, 'No'; 13 and 14, 'Yes'; 15, 'Once or twice'; 16, 'Yes but ...'; 17 to 21, 'No'; 22, 'Yes'; 23 to 25, 'No'.)

Most psychologists agree that our basic nature cannot be changed. However, our ways of functioning can be modified and the key to such modification is self-understanding. What follows is intended to give you objective guidance in this quest.

CHAPTER 16

Upward mobility

Unless you are engaged in a professional activity or in business for yourself you are almost certain to find yourself, sooner or later, involved in three kinds of inter-relationships – with colleagues who are on more or less the same level, with subordinates and with superiors.

We are here concerned chiefly with the nature of your *upward* relations for one simple reason: it is your hierarchical superior who wields the most influence over your destiny within your organisation. Indeed, in a larger sense, your superior's attitude may even affect your entire career, since their opinion of you is likely to be solicited by future prospective employers.

In the course of hundreds of interviews with people from lower, middle and upper management, I have identified the six basic profiles of employee-boss relations that are most frequently encountered. The chances are that you will find that one of them describes your own 'over-under' situation. They are as follows.

THE 'ARM'S-LENGTH' RELATIONSHIP

In this relationship long periods pass without direct face-to-face contact between the individual and the person to whom they report. There may be several reasons for this. Perhaps the superior is 'too busy' to make the necessary time for good communication. Perhaps the employee unconsciously keeps out of reach because of feelings of resentment at any kind of 'interference' with the employee's autonomy. Or the absence of communication may be due, ominously, to the fact that the supervisor is thinking in terms of a 'reorganisation' which would certainly perpetuate the schism. Whatever the reason for the lack of contact, one fact is clear: the individual is flying blind, without real knowledge of what the person they report to thinks of them. (Even if a periodic assessment is a part of the company's practice, no participant in the procedure can count on the cleansing frankness that the designers of the system may have hoped for.)

The dynamic of the 'arm's-length' relation

When all is said and done, there is only one way of knowing what's going on in the mind of your boss. That is to engage the boss in a dialogue. It has been said that misunderstandings grow in proportion to the lack of communication between people. Why is it, then, that we do not insist on frequent meetings with our superiors? After all, logically as well as pragmatically, the maintenance of good communications between the various levels of a hierarchy is in the interest of all – of the individuals involved and, ultimately, of the organisation as a whole.

The explanation of an unwillingness to take the initiative in making contact lies most often, I find, in the early childhood conditioning of many subordinates. Business executives, surveys show, still spring predominantly from middle-class families. From their earliest years, even beyond the reach of memory and continuing through the completion of their studies, a large number of aspiring managers have been the targets of injunctions saying that 'children should be seen and not heard'. When they are indeed listened to, this is generally at the initiative of an adult who, as a consequence of their adulthood, holds power over the youngster – a parent, nurse, teacher. 'I will ask the questions' is the message or 'I will give the instructions'. From that moment on, it is up to 'you' to react (and to react correctly).

What, you may ask, has all this got to do with the behaviour of executives and their staff in the practical matter of advancement in the business world? Just this. For probably more than 20 years of the life of most executives – the 20 most formative years of childhood and adolescence – many such people have been on the receiving end of an unstated agreement between parents and teachers. Both may have conspired, probably unwittingly, to discourage the kind of initiative on the part of children where they demand attention to their needs and aspirations. This is not to say that dialogue itself is always non-existent. When it occurs, however, it is far more likely to have been initiated by the parent (or teacher) than the reverse. Thus the young, developing personality becomes accustomed to a system of one-way communication – from power to relative weakness. To shake off an ingrained habit of such long standing is obviously not an easy task. Is it any wonder then, that so many junior staff hesitate to impinge upon the time of their busy superiors?

Review your own background in the light of your present feelings about the person to whom you report. Was the communication from your parents generally of the 'one-way' nature I have described? Was there a heavy use of parental power to produce that proud possession – a 'good child'? Were you, like most children, frequently asked about your whereabouts, your behaviour and your school work? If so, you may begin to understand a certain reluctance on your part today to knock repeatedly on the office door of your superior in order to initiate a two-way communication.

What can happen when there is only communication from the top down is well illustrated by the experience of Gerald, a client of mine. Gerald had been in military service in the Far East, mostly in Japan, where he became intensely interested in Zen Buddhism. On his discharge he went to work, with responsibilities for client relations, for an important insurance underwriting firm. After 12 years of slow but real progress within his company, he found himself increasingly bored by his job. At the same time his interest in Zen not only continued but grew with the passing years. Putting these two factors together, Gerald decided to explore among insurers the possibility of his working in the Far East. After months of search, he received, to his great joy, an invitation to start up a Hong Kong branch for a company in maritime insurance. He accepted a written proposal and then confronted his general manager to inform him of his decision. The response of his boss staggered Gerald: 'We had no idea you were not satisfied with your job. Why didn't you tell us – especially about your interest in the Orient? It happens that we have plans on the drawing board right now to establish an operation in Japan. You would have been a top candidate for the job.' The final outcome of this conversation was a decision by Gerald to remain with his organisation. But he was forced in great embarrassment to tell the other employer that he would have to break his contract.

In Gerald's case the communications gap ended happily. This is by no means the usual outcome, particularly when the silent one is the boss. I can recall too many clients who, after a lapse of communication, have abruptly found themselves in a meeting that ends in the termination of their employment. 'I had no idea how bad the situation had become,' is a typical comment I hear. Had such people known sooner of the existence of a problem, they could have acted positively; for example, to align their performance more closely to management's needs or to start looking outside the firm.

Efficient senior-junior relations in a business or any other organisation rest on five principles that are readily accepted but far less frequently honoured:

1 the establishment of clear directives by management as to what is expected of the employee;
2 regular feedback to the employee as to the quality of their performance within those directives;
3 opportunities to listen to the feelings and aspirations of the individual;
4 giving the individual the knowledge that they are a 'part of the action' and not just a production tool for the company;
5 assurance of suitable rewards and incentives for good performance.

You will note that all five of these points refer to attitudes and actions that should be provided by management. (Note that they also describe the characteristics of good parenthood.) I suggest that you measure the performance of your management against these criteria. If you conclude that your situation reveals serious shortcomings, you should request a face-to-face discussion with your superior. You may have to persist whether by memo, by telephone or by 'motivating' your superior's secretary to organise a meeting. If this 'putting yourself forward' goes against your nature, do not stop trying. It is very easy to give in to our early directives against importuning authority and thus to sit back, letting days and weeks go by without acting. This is particularly true if the male role model in your childhood (your father) tended to rule by fear and had unpredictable reactions. These lost days and weeks could be precisely those in which decisions are being made over your head, without your knowledge, that could critically affect your future.

What do you say once you are in front of your boss? Perhaps it is too obvious for me to state that you are not there to indict either directly or by implication the actions of management – hardly an approach likely to produce dividends for yourself. Instead, the reasons for your presence are:

1 to request feedback on your performance of your job;
2 to ask if there are new areas of action in which you might help lighten the load carried by the other person;
3 to solicit their views on any important ideas you may have for improving your operations; and
4 (if appropriate) to discuss your possible career evolution in the light of the future development of the company.

Above all, you must not present your boss with operational problems that need to be solved. On this subject the *Manual of Leadership* of the US Navy gives invaluable advice to all seconds-in-command: never present the captain with problems; bring only solutions.

What do you do if you have broached the matter of the lack of communications with goodwill and proactivity, but without achieving a satisfactory conclusion with your superior? In this case, I would not hesitate to recommend a change of job.

Earlier in this chapter, I listed five kinds of situation that can exist apart from the arm's-length relation. Another of the great traps an employee might fall into without realising what is happening is the Parent–Child relationship which is the subject of our next discussion.

THE PARENT–CHILD RELATIONSHIP

Here a lack of communication is not the problem. The superior acts with full control over the junior because that is the actual fact of the matter. An eagerness to please on the part of the subordinate makes them vulnerable to manipulation – so much so that a manipulative boss might be tempted even to keep their distance from time to time simply to nourish feelings of unease in the subordinate. The latter is unlikely to count the hours of the working-week. To be sure, subordinates may count up – with a certain disappointment – their pay, but in their position of servitude they find themselves unable to bring themselves to negotiate an improvement. The nature of the communication in the Parent–Child relationship is again, not surprisingly, one-way – from authority downwards.

The dynamic of the Parent–Child relationship

Among the most dispirited and perplexed of my clients was Martin, a man of 62. For 15 years he had worked with the same company of 500 employees in the manufacture of metal tubing. During those years he had always had the same boss, a charismatic salesperson, and a mover and shaker who had eventually become head of the company. Martin himself had edged up, but only from chief of general services to a vaguely defined post of general secretary. Even by the time I met him, Martin's salary had never kept pace with his education, his real abilities or with his title. Now he was tired – 'wrung out', as he put it – but without the chance of taking early retirement because his modest salary had prevented him saving anything.

Early in his talks with me Martin identified his problem as one of 'loyalty'. He explained that over the years he had devoted all of his energy, all of his thoughts and nearly all of his time to the support of his president. Two-day weekends were a rarity and Martin's wife complained bitterly of his habitually late arrival for dinner. She also complained that throughout his career Martin had always given far more of himself to his employers than he received in return. Finally, and much too late, his own promptings, along with his wife's urgings, had culminated in a decision to leave his company for a new job. At Martin's age the search was not easy but at last a company saw him as the bargain he in fact was and agreed to employ him as head of its small administrative department until Martin reached retirement age three years later. It was what executive search firms euphemistically call a 'lateral promotion'.

Unfortunately, Martin's story is not an unusual one. Intelligent, well educated, morally impeccable, he found himself on a kind of career treadmill without real satisfaction and without the advancement that his merits warranted. He was repeatedly 'used' and ultimately, almost too late, he woke up to the fact. It required no psychologist to help Martin recognise the causes that lay behind his ineffectual use of his qualities. The sudden death of his father in a car accident when he was four years old turned out to have been the key event in Martin's life. An only child, he was informed repeatedly by his mother of the great and noble qualities of the husband she mourned. Even before the start of his career, Martin was in search of a substitute father among his teachers and lecturers. For some of them he found he could work at a level exceeding his usual capacities; for others, the reverse was true. Later on, superiors who were successful due to their firmness, intelligence and attractive personalities were able to gain his loyalty. Praise gave him a kind of inner satisfaction he had thirsted for in his childhood. Criticism from superiors sent him into depression and caused him to redouble his efforts to prove himself worthy.

Women as well as men can be affected by the early loss of a father. However, the effect is likely to be different. Since the parent of the opposite sex can never be a complete model of behaviour, such a loss for a woman is likely to produce the feeling of having been abandoned by her original protector and mentor. The result can be resentment, well or ill concealed, against what she perceives to be untrustworthy male bosses.

The death of the male parent is, of course, not the only circumstance that may cause a person to seek a surrogate father. Some fathers are absent because they are married to their work. Others are effectively absent because of age or illness. Still others might just as well be absent because of their weakness in carrying out the responsibilities of fatherhood. Whatever its cause, the absence we are speaking of leaves a void which is unconsciously felt by the sons of such fathers and which, once filled by an acceptable model of authority, leaves the individual vulnerable to the manipulations of the dominant person. Obviously from the point of view of the adopted 'parent', the eagerness to please on the part of the junior is not without its benefits. With the best will conceivable, the senior cannot help but see their role as that of a person who has a job to do – one that is performed largely through using other people. To have at hand a person who is very ready to do anything asked is not only a great convenience but also provides a gratifying boost to their own self-esteem.

Even a cursory glance at the dynamic of the Parent–Child relationship reveals that it is a fraud. The younger person could get worn out trying to perform tasks that, in the interest of real efficiency, rightly should be handled by more than one person. An over-worked, over-stressed person is no more efficient than an over-taxed machine and the end result in either case can be permanent damage. Moreover, superiors sometimes change companies, retire or die. In the kind of relationship we are looking at, such a loss is traumatic for the employee, who faces, once again, the problem of finding a substitute parent. And the 'superior' may also unwittingly become the victim of a certain kind of dependency. In relying on a hierarchical style of management, from unquestioned authority downward, the superior is liable to get badly out of step with the accepted principles of modern, participative management. The time could well arrive when the boss cannot find anyone willing to subject themselves to this particular brand of parental dynamism and will have to reorganise their attitudes towards delegation and participation.

The role of fear

In Parent–Child relationships, fear is almost always a factor. It is hardly surprising that at the outset of life a physically small, essentially helpless person should feel awe at their parents' relatively immense size and power. Whether they are active or latent, feelings of fear on the part of the child will have, of course, much to do with their obedience to the parents' wishes. Most business psychologists agree that a person's early conditioning inside the family unit is likely to be reflected later on in their way of responding to the dynamics of human relations at work.

Certain managers habitually use fear as a way to spur employees to greater effort. Some years ago I was in the office of Frederick B, the founder and chief officer of a well-known investment counselling firm. Suddenly, in the course of our conversation about employee relations, he asked me what I considered to be the most important motivator of people in organisations. I forget my precise answer, though no doubt it had to do with feelings of participation and growth on the part of employees.

'Not at all', Mr B replied. 'It is fear that gets the maximum results.'

Outside his office Mr B came across as an older man of great charm who seemed in every way to fit the description of a 'gentleman'. Yet few members of his team entered his office without feelings of terror. No action on their part was likely to win approval. Personal weaknesses were probed with surgical skill. Errors were rebuked with a cold and devastating fury.

Mr B's answer to his own question did not entirely surprise me, since I had already been in touch with members of his staff, all of whom had to be reassured that I would preserve their anonymity. It was in speaking with these people that I earned why they stayed with the company. First of all Mr B paid well – so that his people were unlikely to be able to match their salary level on the outside. Secondly, as boss he had their respect. He was the smartest and best among them, and they knew it; as such he was a person from whom they could and did learn constantly.

From this story, one conclusion is clear. The boss who habitually uses fear must be competent or risk disaster. If, like Mr B, the boss actually does have superior abilities, the danger to any employee seeking a controlling 'parent' is evident. The factors of admiration, a decent financial reward and displayed power all combine to lure the unwary into a kind of bondage from which it is not easy to escape. Unfortunately many who do so make their exit, not voluntarily, but as a result of burn-out.

The admiring parent

Just as some people are motivated by fear and power, others bloom under admiration. This fact does not escape the notice of a certain kind of surrogate parent. I am thinking of, among others, the learning experience of Bruce M, the manager until recently of the Belgian subsidiary of an American company in the field of hospital equipment. His job was often a lonely one due to its remoteness from the central action of the company back home. Due to the absence of professional management contact and communication, he was surprised when he received word that the parent company was about to be acquired by a larger group.

Not long afterwards Bruce received a visit from the treasurer of the company that had purchased his own, a man who was reputed to be the closest adviser to the group president. His visitor's admiration for the very real progress of the Belgian subsidiary was unconcealed, as was his appreciation for the good rapport that Bruce had built up in his team. Other visits followed, marked by similar verbal and non-verbal messages of approval. Between the two men there grew a remarkable mutual understanding.

Finally, at the end of Bruce's time in Brussels, he was brought back to New York with the vague title of assistant general manager. He found himself reporting, predictably, not to the treasurer but to a vice-president who happened to be in spirited, though unpublicised, competition with the other man. From that point on Bruce's working life became a series of monotonous chores, punctuated by long periods of under-utilisation that were difficult for his active nature to accept. To Bruce this treatment was a mystery until a friend in the personnel department squared with him. 'You've been away too long, Bruce. Don't you realise that your case is being pushed by the treasurer and so the vice-president senses that your real loyalty belongs to the treasurer? The trouble is, the vice-president has power, while the treasurer is staff with limited clout. Sorry, but you've got a tough selling job to do if you're going to break through.' He thought a moment, then added, 'Impossible, I'd say.' Time proved the personnel man to be right and finally Bruce decided to look elsewhere.

We have here a story that illustrates exactly the reverse of the hypnotic effect of fear. In this case, the putative 'superior' – the treasurer – was seeking an ally to help him widen his sphere of power beyond his largely staff role. He knew that a person distanced from their home base, working with little recognition of his accomplishments, was in some respects like a neglected child whose merits go unnoticed and unappreciated. This is the factor that gave the older man his fraudulent hold on Bruce. (I use the word 'fraudulent' to make the point that this kind of relationship – like others described in this chapter – does not have as its chief goal the well-being of the enterprise, but rather the satisfaction of certain individual psychological drives.)

A junior member of staff should speculate on the motives of a senior who is overly attentive, particularly if the person is not in a direct supervisory relationship. Granted, it is not easy to ignore hard-won approval and, in fact, there is no reason to reject it. To maintain good contact only makes sense. However, to dedicate a major share of your loyalty to someone who might not be able to match their actions to their words does not.

THE OLDER SIBLING RELATIONSHIP

Here we have the ideal of many younger managers. More common in smaller than in larger companies, the older sibling relationship is as close to equality as is possible within a vertical company structure. The boss does not act like a boss, but more like a leader – a leader who is able to establish two-way communication with a subordinate, who corrects without chastising, whose door is open in times of need. Since nothing is perfect in either the corporate or any other world, there is an evident danger here: when such a boss is transferred, retired or, for any other reason, is no longer present, the subordinate faces the problem of finding a similar rare bird – of undertaking a possibly fruitless search for a comparable model.

The dynamic of the older sibling relationship

The dream of many junior executives is to work under someone who is older and more experienced, but who sees the junior as an equal, asking the junior's views on future actions and explaining the reasons for decisions once taken. Such a person can rule lightly but firmly, relying more on example than on precept, providing frequent feedback to the junior and offering defence from criticism when things go wrong, as they inevitably sometimes do.

Given such an ideal over–under relationship, why should I include this in my collection of fraudulent relationships? Again, I can best illustrate the point by citing the situation of a former client of mine. This person, Adrian M was the brilliant son of the headmaster of one of England's best known private schools. Adrian himself graduated from Cambridge with honours in engineering, before joining the headquarters of a major British oil company as a trainee.

Ten years later he requested a meeting with me. I found myself facing a puzzled and dejected research assistant, frustrated by his lack of progress in his career. We talked about his early development as is my custom, including some discussion of his relationship with his father. Here we found a clue to Adrian's career problems. While his father's principal office was in the administration building of the school, he frequently worked at home. At such times his door was open to Adrian, more and more so as Adrian progressed into his teens. During their chats in the father's book-lined library, they met almost as equals, the one speaking of his problems with the faculty and the administration of the school, the other of his difficulties with certain teachers. Adrian never had to beg for attention and was never given the impression that he was wasting his father's time. Instead his father's way was to treat Adrian as an adult, but none the less one for whom he had a continued responsibility. In his attitude there were similarities to the ideal role of a caring older brother.

At the time of our meeting, Adrian was 33 years old, tall, fit, with a thoughtful but pleasant face and an easy way of relating to people. His career, after his selection as a trainee, was satisfying, if not spectacular, up to three years earlier. At that time, his boss, the head of research, retired. Like Adrian's father, this person had been a 'brain'. At the same time he was open and communicative, available and always supportive – like a caring big brother. This similarity between the behaviour of his boss and his father turned out to be the explanation of the flat course Adrian's career had taken after the boss retired. There was no need in his mind to put himself forward, to knock on doors. Why do so? After all, it was his experience that the doors to higher levels opened automatically. Subsequently when his 'brotherly' superior left the company for another job, this continued to be Adrian's expectation. Little by little, however, he came to see that he was in danger of becoming lost in the faceless crowd of younger executives moving up from the trainee level as he himself had done several years before.

Together we worked out a programme whereby Adrian would behave more proactively within his company, letting it be known in the right places that he was indeed motivated and ready, despite his earlier appearance of contentment, to tackle greater responsibilities. Within a short time Adrian moved into product management and the career block was removed.

The moral of this story? While the kind of relationship with power that Adrian had become accustomed to is a comfortable one; this very fact carries with it the risk that it might become a seductive kind of trap. There is an American saying that a squeaking wheel gets the most oil. If you find yourself under the wing of an 'older sibling' you may have little reason to complain or squeak, but at the same time you are in a real sense a prisoner, albeit a willing prisoner, of your situation. Since proactivity on your own behalf has not been required of you, you are deprived of practice in projecting your best qualities to others – in other words, in 'selling yourself'. In one sense, Adrian was lucky; after the first 'older sibling' (his father) he found a substitute (his boss). In another sense he was unlucky since the mutual satisfaction that existed between his boss and himself served to cause him to lag behind his colleagues in his progression within the company.

The problem of the older sibling is not likely to produce easy, open-and-shut answers that apply universally for the simple reason that some people don't see any problem in this kind of relationship. They find a transaction that satisfies them as long as it lasts. When it ends they simply await the opening of another door into a similarly sooth-ing sibling relationship. However, such passivity – waiting for 'some-thing to happen' – does not fit with the ideas expressed in this book which are:

- that there is a drive for advancement and self-realisation within most people;
- that within most organisations such evolution can only be ensured by an attitude of 'proactivity' rather than passivity.

One thing is clear. Frequently there is a choice to be made between comfort and progress. Within the dynamic of the older sibling rela-tionship, either choice – to stay within the relationship as long as possible or to opt out after a reasonable period of time – can be justified. The important thing, however, is that the choice should be made consciously, after weighing up the pros and cons, rather than blindly as the result of a comfortable complacency. If the latter is in control, you may find you have serious regrets later on.

THE YOUNG TURK, OLD GUARD RELATIONSHIP

In this era of MBAs, it often happens that a younger person amply armed with modern management tools ends up reporting to an older person whose rise has been more due to success in the rough-and-tumble of competition at work than to academic achievement. Here there can be a communications gap, but not necessarily because of an absence of contact. The problem frequently has to do with the vul-nerability/sensitivity of the boss, who may feel vulnerable in discus-sions with a supposed 'inferior' whose knowledge in some ways may in fact surpass that of the boss. The result is a confusion in the boss's self-image ('Am I really over the hill?') and a consequent danger that the boss will become overbearing in trying to reinforce their authority. In turn, the younger person may interpret – in some cases correctly – the superior's attitude as representing outdated hierarchical management at its most virulent. The possibility of an explosion between the threatened ego of the boss and the latent contempt of the junior is all too apparent.

The dynamic of the young Turk, old guard relationship

Little heeded is the fact that the 1980s marked a quiet revolution in the executive offices of the Western world. The post-war bosses were on their way out. A young person of 18 caught up in the Second World War in 1940 would have reached a normal, perhaps obligatory, retirement age of 65 in 1987. Millions of such people were sidetracked by the war for a number of years – from their education and/or from their career. In 1945 life began again with a tremendous reconstructive release of energy on the part of the fittest of youth worldwide. All were seeking their place in the sun. Some of them founded small businesses of their own (not all of these remained small). Others entered into existing companies to begin a competitive struggle made all the keener by the awareness of the years that had been lost. Today, however, they have been and are being replaced by younger people with an experience of life that is quite different from their own.

Except for those who took part in localised wars, spread over a period of 15 years, the post Second World War generations in the Northern countries grew up unscarred either by a major depression or a great war. For them money was easier to come by than for their parents and so, consequently, was the possibility of higher education. The first degree that was the ultimate prize usually sought by the older generation became a minimum entry requirement to the good jobs of the 1960s and '70s.

Given their very different backgrounds, it is not surprising that the change from the old guard to the new has not always been an easy one. The case of Alex illustrates the point. In the early 1980s he was recruited as number 2 to the president of a company manufacturing floor coverings and employing 3 000 people. One of the factors that motivated Alex to leave his good job as financial director of an important textile company was the businesslike way the president of his new company conducted his search for a successor. With the aid of a reputable executive search firm a precise profile of the post had been established, along with a clear statement of the responsibilities to be assumed by the new recruit. In brief, the company sought top qualifications (such as Alex's masters' degree) and was willing to pay for them.

Furthermore, his direct contacts with the president impressed Alex. This was a man of charisma, equipped with a keen mind, who showed the good sense to plan for his retirement three years ahead of the event. Unfortunately Alex was not long with the company before doubts began to enter his mind. Yes, this was beyond doubt a brilliant president, but the 'methods' that controlled the company all seemed to exist only in his head. When Alex tried to talk of zero-based budgeting, the matrix system, management by objectives or quality circles his boss listened, then usually asked for a 'memorandum' on the subject. As the memos piled up without action the profit figures of the company continued a downward spiral that had set in well before Alex's arrival.

Worse still, something was happening to the relationship between the older and the younger man. Each time Alex pressed for reform, the president responded with words like 'theoretical', 'academic' and 'impractical'. For his part Alex began to discern that the open-mindedness he had admired in the other was nothing but a well-practised sham. Irritated, he felt like a dupe and at times thought that his loss of respect for his boss was beginning to show. The end finally came when the president let it be known that, as principal stockholder of the company, he planned to exercise his right not to retire after all at the time he had programmed. He gave no specific reason for this change but said to others that he felt his intended successor was not quite ready to assume the heavy responsibilities involved. Tired of waiting and despairing of trying to open a closed mind, Alex went back to the executive search firm that had placed him in his job. The head of the firm said correctly that to help Alex find a new post elsewhere would have been contrary to the practices of his profession. Alex then quit his job and began a search that dragged out over six painful months.

The story of Alex took place at the top levels of management of a smaller company. But similar differences of perception between the generations can exist at every level of management – from the shop floor to general headquarters. So long as power and authority remain in the hands of the 'old guard', the responsibility for maintaining the best possible communications rests, whether they like it or not, with the newer arrivals. It is probably no easier for them to put themselves in the shoes of the older person than vice versa. None the less, it is only by trying to understand the feelings of their elders that the 'new guard' can hope to become a part of an orderly transition. In doing so, however taxing the process may be, they can at least console themselves that the future belongs to them. In such situations, a certain amount of patience may prove to be the minimum ransom necessary for moving upwards.

Sometimes the reverse of the situation described above is even more difficult. Here the younger person, who has already worked their way up to a post of command, becomes the boss of one or more older people. To help either party in such a relationship to understand the psychological factors involved, I also recommend a study of transactional analysis and perhaps even participation in a TA seminar. As we have seen, with its clear delineation of the 'Parent', 'Adult' and 'Child' that exist within the personality of each of us, this technique has become a standard – almost classical – tool within many corporations for improving human relations.

When we assume a 'parental' attitude, often using didactic words like 'should', 'ought' and 'must', we are almost certain to rub up the wrong way people who see themselves rightly or wrongly – due to their age, position or seniority – as entitled to assume a parental role. Conversely, when we behave, in psychological terms, like a 'child', assenting to whatever proposition authority puts forward (or rebelling against it instinctively), we run the risk of finding ourselves in the 'Parent–Child' trap. To steer clear of the Charybdis of the 'Parent' and the Scylla of the 'Child', our use of the 'Adult' – the rational, objective faculty of our make-up – offers solid ground on which to base a move forwards into the future.

THE OVERLAPPING RELATIONSHIP

Perhaps as a consequence of the management style of the superior, occasionally as a result of some real or imagined shortcoming of the subordinate, an overlapping of functions can be among the most troublesome of hierarchical relations. A boss may show a lack of confidence in an employee through constant interference in the execution of the details of jobs supposedly delegated to the junior. The major cause of such behaviour is an innate inability on the part of the higher executive to put trust in the capabilities of others. The fallout is likely to damage both persons – the boss who may be diverting managerial time to tasks of secondary importance (thereby, incidentally, stunting their own growth), but especially to the subordinate who is deprived of the chance to test their wings. Also, the subordinate must possess an unusually high level of self-confidence in order to avoid being contaminated by the superior's evident lack of regard for the subordinate's abilities.

The dynamic of the overlapping relationship

Three types of overlapping relationships are commonly found in all types of organisations – companies whose objective is to earn money, non-governmental organisations whose mission is other than profit-making and institutions whose source of financing is the taxpayer. Within any of these structures, two people can sometimes be found occupying themselves with similar functions for any one of the following reasons.

- As we have already seen, a senior in authority lacks confidence in the abilities of a junior and therefore the senior person interferes in the day-to-day activity of the subordinate.

- A third person is parachuted into the organisation between a senior and the senior's immediate subordinate.

- A 'dotted line' relationship has been established so that each key executive in a subsidiary finds themselves reporting not only to the chief executive officer of the subsidiary but also to a person at headquarters. Typical of this kind of double reporting is the case of financial officers whose direct responsibility may be to the manager of a local subsidiary, but who also have a reporting relationship with the chief financial officer of the parent company.

The first of these three situations is fraught with dangers for the future of the subordinate and if you are in this position you must demand an urgent meeting with your superior. Only two possibilities exist here: either the boss lacks confidence in the employee or the boss is among those people who have trouble letting go – in other words, in delegating work to others. In either of these cases, it might not be easy to arrange a frank discussion. If the boss lacks confidence in you, they might fear that an open acknowledgement of any doubts could further damage your performance. If the difficulty is due to the fact that the boss cannot delegate to others, this can only mean that the superior is not a good executive – a conclusion that the superior will be loath to admit to.

Given these two built-in barriers to discussion, you will probably have to push hard for a meeting. If the problem does turn out to be a real lack of confidence in your own performance, you have the right to ask about the exact nature of the reservations harboured by the other person. Of prime importance in such a discussion is to arrive at a clear understanding of the areas of improvement sought by your boss.

The second overlapping situation – that caused by the insertion of a newcomer between yourself and the boss – should be seen as a red flashing warning signal. No matter how such a change is presented – as a 'restructuring', as a 'division of responsibilities' due to expansion or as a newly created 'staff function' – the direct communication that there was between boss and employee is likely thereafter to be diluted or ruptured completely. In such a situation, you may find that a face-to-face meeting with your superior is unlikely to be productive.

This was the case with Bill B, who moved up from marketing director to the post of assistant managing director of his leather goods company soon after the company was taken over by a diversified group.

Because the new managing director had been parachuted from the financial department of the parent company, he had no knowledge whatsoever of the leather business. As a result he leaned for several months on Bill's know-how in the field. One day, just as Bill was beginning to feel that the worst of the trauma of the merger was over, a 'consultant' appeared as the occupant of an office next to the managing director's. From that day on, contact between Bill and his boss became less and less frequent. Worse, Bill increasingly found himself encountering the 'consultant' in conference in the offices of certain department heads who were nominally reporting to Bill.

Then the day arrived when Bill was told that the production quota for a certain line of pocket diaries had been reduced without his knowledge. On learning that the order had come 'from the managing director's office', Bill demanded a meeting with him. In reply to his protest, the MD said:

'I think you are being a little too sensitive. You have to understand that this company can only move forward with the benefit of really professional management. Roger [the consultant] has had a wide range of experience in top companies and I find that we need that. Our existing people are – how can I put it? – necessarily narrow in their outlook.'

Weeks later Roger himself appeared in Bill's office. The number of members of management, he declared, were clearly out of line with accepted ratios. For this reason the managing director had decided that the post of assistant could and should be eliminated. Since there obviously existed no other slot for Bill at a comparable level in the organisation, Roger 'understood' that the MD was prepared to terminate Bill's contract on 'very favourable terms'. Wisely Bill saw no way to do battle with a managing director who was hiding behind his emissary. In the end he negotiated a settlement that give him enough cash to finance the creation of a small business of his own.

The matrix system

The third danger of overlapping functions lies in the nature of the relations between the management of a subsidiary and the direction of the parent company. Fearful that the growth of their subsidiaries might make them overly independent, a number of companies have decided to take back into their headquarters the real control of the various units of the group. The result is often called the 'matrix system', meaning that the heads of the departments of each subsidiary – such as finance, sales or production – report directly to their hierarchical counterpart at headquarters. The result can be and often is an overlap between local management and centralised control. The department heads in the subsidiary now find they have in effect two bosses – one locally and another at headquarters. The person who formerly had full local responsibility inevitably feels diminished in stature, but can also end up dealing with matters that are already being handled directly between one of the so-called subordinates and a superior back at home base.

As with the situation faced by Bill, here we again find that no amount of dialogue is likely to restore the situation of the person who was formerly fully responsible for the operations of a subsidiary. That person really only has two alternatives. The first is to seek a new post in another organisation which offers clear responsibility. The second is to hang on until the company wearies of the problem inherent in centralised control and decides to return its authority back to the subsidiary. Over the years I have seen the pendulum swing back and forth between centralised and decentralised control. None the less the danger of opting for a waiting game is obvious. Managers who no longer have the full scope of authority for which they are paid can well be regarded as a luxury by their employers. Then, too, not all of the companies with experience in 'matrixing' will want to reverse their course. In any case, such a decision may be a long time coming, especially in the perception of people caught up in an overlapping relationship.

Confusing as the situation can be for the top person in the subsidiary unit, this problem is frequently shared by the key people in the various local departments. They also may be uncertain as to who is the boss. Is the black line linking them with the local manager more weighty than the dotted line back to headquarters? The response will vary in different situations. If you find yourself on this level, you will study the attitudes of visiting executives from the home office. If they tend to brush aside the boss of your unit, and to deal directly with you and your colleagues, you are well advised to orient your future communications accordingly. If, for reasons of loyalty or general principle, such a reorientation goes against the grain, you may want to think in terms of a change to a differently structured organisation, where the lines of authority are more clearly defined.

THE PROFESSIONAL RELATIONSHIP

What, precisely, is the real meaning of the word 'professional'? My own definition is a simple one. The professional is a person whose concentration is directed towards obtaining the best possible results in their work. Thus, neither party in a truly professional relationship is draining their energies in order to satisfy a fraudulent psychological need – the kind of need that pioneering psychologist Alfred Adler identified as basically non-productive and selfish in nature. A true search for perfection by both members of a professional boss–employee team is almost certain to be a source of fruitful combined action rather than the reverse. And here I am speaking of the enrichment of the individuals involved, as well as the enterprise of which they are a part.

The dynamic of the professional relationship

When speaking of a professional relationship in its purest form, many people almost automatically visualise a surgeon in action. No external factor can be allowed to come between the professional and the goal to which they are dedicated – the return to health of the patient. Whatever troubles the professional may have at home, whatever the harassment or other ongoing concerns, all thoughts and feelings tangential to the work at hand must be put aside.

In fact such pure professionalism is rarely found in organisational life and neither is it, in most cases, to be desired. When people are forced to work together for a common goal, human feelings are bound to play an important – perhaps decisive – role. The aim, thus, of the professional should be not to avoid the professional's and others' feelings, but to recognise them in order to understand the forces underlying them.

Below you will find six questions that can help you test the nature of your communications in the six types of hierarchical relationships we have discussed in this chapter. Your answers will help you to see your own way of behaving in 'over–under' situations more objectively.

	Yes	No

1 Am I finding the real rewards of my work primarily in satisfying my need for the approval of a super-boss, a surrogate parent?

2 Am I continually under-utilised because I am hoping some day to be invited into a comfortable older sibling arrangement with a boss, instead of behaving proactively to advance my position and influence?

3 Am I jeopardizing my future because of aggressive feelings aroused in the course of a young Turk, old guard relationship?

4 Am I feeling discouraged, perhaps even abandoned, because another person has won the preference of my boss?

5 Am I feeling diminished because another person has pre-empted a part of the functions that normally should be performed by me?

6 Is my effectiveness and my satisfaction in my role not only undiminished by my relations with my boss, but rather enhanced by a sense of common goals, openness of communication and respect for my boss's demonstrated qualities as a leader?

If your answer to the first five questions is 'No' and to question 6 is 'Yes', you can honestly say that you are working within a truly professional relationship – in other words that you are in a position of synergy. On the other hand, a 'Yes' to any one of the first five questions calls for a re-examination of your situation – first of your own way of behaving, then of that of others and ultimately, perhaps, of the desirability of making a change within or outside your organisation.

However, we should at the same time be aware that the old hierarchical structures are crumbling. An executive no longer can progress solely because of an ability to strike the right employee–boss relationship. Instead your effectiveness is increasingly the result of your success in bringing people together – in other words, in motivating groups in a collective effort.

We must, in short, be very aware of the sources of lateral synergy – the subject of the next chapter.

CHAPTER 17

Lateral relationships

PART1: ONE-TO-ONE EXCHANGES

While the manner with which we handle 'over–under', or hierarchical, relationships is often crucial to career progress, as we have seen, the same is also true in our relationships with our peers. This is especially true today as enterprises place increasing emphasis on co-operation, team work and group decisions.

Our communications with people on the same level as ourselves customarily take two forms – encounters between individuals and encounters in group meetings. First we will look at one-to-one interchanges and later at the very special complexities of group interactivity.

It is easy to say that in our relationships with others we should be serious, but not too serious, that we should strive for a 'professional' relationship rather than make close friends of our collaborators, that we should be open and friendly while still not forgetting that colleagues can also be competitors. We may agree to such principles and yet at the same time realise that they leave out an element that is all too present in corporate life. This is 'office politics'.

Sometimes the manipulations that come under the heading of office politics are not very pleasant. Clearly, I have no intention of producing a manual on how to become an office politician. What I am aiming to do is help the many able executives who – at least in the early stages of their careers – have been taught to believe that hard work, intelligence and openness are the only ways to advance. Often they learn, too late and to their regret, that this is not the case. The missing quality can be described, not as aggressive office politics, but rather as *defensive* politics – the ability to discern and therefore to disarm the real motivations of certain people around us. With one small modification the New Testament describes best the ideal attitude: to be 'as wise as serpents and [outwardly] harmless as doves'.

We can generalise by saying that the larger the organisation, the more executive time is devoted to 'political' activity. However, I can point to situations in smaller organisations where able people have suddenly found that someone has suddenly and surprisingly moved into a position they thought they were destined to fill. To help avoid such unpleasant surprises, I have compiled a series of examples of how some colleagues of clients of mine have turned out to be anything but 'friendly competitors'. My hope is that these case histories (some of them horror stories) will serve as a warning against falling victim to similar machinations.

'I never mix business with my social life'

This was the firm credo of Oliver P, a member of the board of directors of a company of 2 000 people in the linen supply business. The board surrounded the president of the firm like so many satellites of equal weight and size. Because Oliver's particular responsibility was marketing and sales he was often out of the office. None the less, he felt secure in his job for two reasons: first, because his performance was excellent when judged by the revenue increases the company was showing; and secondly because of the warm relationship between the chairman and himself, cemented over a period of 12 years. When Oliver came to see me he started out by saying that he thought he was going stale, that his job had lost its savour and that he felt it was time to change companies.

Only after an hour of conversation did the real reason for his low morale become clear. The chairman had called him into his office a week earlier to announce that one of his colleagues, the person in charge of finance, was to be named general manager with responsibilities for the overall functioning of the organisation. Oliver was staggered by the news and could not understand the promotion of his associate over his head. However, the mystery was at least partly dispelled when I learned that the chairman and Oliver's associate belonged to the same golf club, and that their wives frequently joined them there for lunch and on other social occasions. This information made it clear that the new director had been able to establish a dimension in his relationship with the president from which Oliver, by choice, had excluded himself.

This is not to say that Oliver's choice was a 'wrong' one. What is clear, however, is that Oliver failed to foresee the consequences to his career of a rigid separation between his work and his social life. He did not 'read' his chairman's need for companionship as well as for pragmatism in his relationships with others. Even if he had been in possession of such information, Oliver might still have decided to compartmentalise his life, even taking into account the possible limitation he was placing on his chances of career advancement. In his case, his choice of lifestyle was made blindly, in ignorance of the risk factor involved. Not surprisingly, the consequences came as a rude shock.

THE MORAL: **Decide what you really want from life but don't be surprised if you get it.**

'Let's lunch together'

Edward A was surprised when the head of marketing made the suggestion, thinking that probably he himself should have taken the initiative. As chief of the environmental protection section of an important household products company, he was the senior colleague, but it simply had not occurred to him to act first, so with a certain sense of guilt he went along with the idea. At the end of the meal, the marketing manager showed Edward a letter he had received from an executive search firm. As is customary the letter did not suggest directly that the recipient might be a candidate for the post in question but asked, rather, if he 'knew of anyone who might be interested'. The job was important – head of research for a large international company in toiletries – but not at all suited to the marketing manager.

'I thought you might want to do a favour for someone you know by telling him about the opening,' he said. Actually Edward himself was fascinated by the job description which fitted him perfectly, but he thought it better not to communicate his interest to his luncheon companion. That evening he started to work on a résumé to send off to the 'head hunter'. He kept the first draft of this document, as well as a covering letter, in his briefcase in order to polish up a few points during the days to come.

Three days later he received a summons to the office of the managing director. 'I am sure you know the policy of this company regarding our executives who are looking for opportunities elsewhere.' Edward did indeed know. Such people were invited to leave the organisation. Within minutes he himself received just such an invitation after having been shown a photocopy of his résumé and letter. 'I'm really sorry about this,' said the managing director, 'but I have no choice. Policy is policy. As to your own habits, may I simply suggest that in your future post you do not leave your briefcase unguarded.'

Edward, of course, never learned who had raided his briefcase.

What he did realise was that only one person in the organisation knew that he had in his possession a description of a position to be filled.

THE MORAL: **The managing director said it best at the end of his meeting with Edward.**

'I never felt so alone'

That was the way Sam G summed up his feelings after the management buy-out of his company. For reasons that we set out to examine together he had not been invited to join the group of employees who made a successful leveraged bid for the shares of his employer in the business of manufacturing for the semi-conductors industry. He felt, with reason, that his position as production manager of three plants placed him on a level with the other department heads who had joined together without him. Tracing back Sam's history I learned that he had graduated in engineering from an undistinguished college and had plunged directly into plant management, working his way up from a modest start in quality control. He was a happy man. He adored machinery and when automated production came into vogue, he was fascinated by the introduction of robotics into his work spaces. What did not interest him was the starchy atmosphere of headquarters. He spent most of his time on the shop floors, dressed in jeans and always ready to take up a screwdriver when there was a problem. His men revered him and Sam ate in their canteen, sometimes drank with them after work, and met their wives and families whenever the occasion presented itself. Over the years he cemented an image of himself as a 'worker' rather than as an 'executive'.

Apart from his hurt at not being invited to join in the management takeover, I am certain that Sam was a happier man than most of the 'in-group'. It is true that his career had reached a plateau, but even with prior knowledge would he have changed? I doubt it. His history is that of many managers whose relationship with 'the guys' was unchanging during successive promotions. His preference for their companionship and for the shop floor cut him off from real communication with his peers in headquarters, but at the same time it had a lot to do with his effectiveness in his job. He was not offended when he finally came to realise that he had been typecast in headquarters, not as management, but more as 'one of the people in the workshop'. He simply shrugged. 'If that's the price I have to pay for having fun in my job, I'm ready to pay it.' Not all managers are so philosophical when they find themselves marked down by their colleagues due to their loyalty to their subordinates rather than upwards in the organisation. Many simply are not willing to pay the price, but pay it they must, none the less.

THE MORAL: **Don't expect to be invited to tea with the bosses if you are always drinking beer with the boys.**

'How can I help?'

New to the company, Phil W was touched when, within hours of his arrival, Bradley, the chief of logistics, came to see him to offer any assistance he could give to help Phil find his way around the company. This was an appropriate gesture, in any case, since Bradley was the purchasing director for this international manufacturer of air conditioning equipment, and their roles meshed closely. Since that first day, the two men found enough time together for Bradley to give Phil the lowdown on all of the key people in the organisation. Phil was particularly glad to have Bradley's warning about the director of operations, who was situated just above both of them on the organisation chart. 'Be careful. Try to avoid dealing with him in the morning,' was Bradley's advice. When Phil asked why, Bradley coughed and then said, 'Well, he's not in his finest shape before lunch, if you follow me.' Phil knew that Bradley was hinting at the existence of a drinking problem but saw no reason to press the point. However, in the course of Bradley's introductions of Phil to other members of the organisation, Phil was struck by the number of times the same warning was repeated. He decided whenever possible to meet with the operations manager in the afternoon. For a period of time he managed to do so, but there came a Monday morning when his boss summoned him for a meeting at 8.30. He was surprised at the time proposed and even more surprised during the meeting to find himself confronting a man in great form – friendly, incisive, dynamic.

This experience prompted Phil to check out another scrap of 'intelligence' received from Bradley and his circle. According to them, the general manager of the company and his secretary were getting on so well together that many of the general manager's trips to exotic places were in her company and were for purposes that could be called anything but strictly business. Phil made it a point to get to know the secretary (a good thing to do in any case) and soon learned that she was widowed with three children at home, one of them disabled. It was evident that her life was so centred on her family that the mere idea of romantic excursions with her boss was wildly improbable. Other similar discrepancies between rumour and fact followed in succession. Phil soon saw the truth – that he had fallen in with a rebellious group, intent on bringing him into their anti-management circle. He detached himself from the group with as much diplomacy as possible and went on to cement himself solidly into the management team. The moral to Phil's story is not that we must reject an outstretched hand, but to do as he did; that is, to move warily before being made a captive of any private clique inside the company structure.

THE MORAL: **At the beginning of a new job, take care not to be adopted by the guerrillas.**

'In writing? Why, we are all friends here!'

A minor North American manufacturer of agricultural equipment was seeking a director of sales and marketing for the US, its most important region. Joseph F was contacted in Germany by the company's executive search firm, because of his regional sales experience with a larger manufacturer. An American and eager to return to the US Joe went to London for a series of interviews with the 'head hunter' and a preliminary interview with the company's director of sales. Not only was the job profile interesting, but the salary offered was 30 per cent above what he was currently earning. Finally Joe was brought to the US for a meeting with the company president. Together they worked out a package of compensation that Joe felt he could not refuse. In accepting the offer, he said that he would await the arrival of a written contract before giving his final decision. The president seemed shocked.

'But you don't understand how our company functions,' he said. He went on to explain that teamwork was the essence of management's cohesiveness. 'We don't want anyone here to feel they are the prisoner of a written document. Nor do we wish to have our speed and flexibility hampered by a lot of legaleze. Either we can work together in good faith and in harmony or we'd prefer not to work together at all.' Joe pointed out that he would be leaving a good job, that he had a wife and two children to care for, and that he felt he needed certain protection. 'Our word is your best protection,' was the answer. 'Without mutual confidence and respect I'm sure you'll agree that documents are worthless.' Joe liked the man and he liked the other future collaborators he had met. This fact, coupled with the attractive salary and title, and with his wife's desire to get back to America, led Joe (against my advice) to accept the post. Eight months later he was back in my office. The company's figures had gone sour. Panic had siezed the board of directors. His job had been eliminated – as was he himself, without notice, as the most recent new executive to come aboard. After a very tough passage, Joe found an acceptable position. But I am certain that during the rest of his career, he would never again allow his idealism to blind him to the pragmatic realities of the business world.

THE MORAL: **Even when joining what is supposedly 'one big happy family', it's wise to 'get it in writing'.**

'There were two warring camps'

However, Frank R didn't know that. Perhaps he was too carried away at first by the fact that he had sold an idea to the president of the publishing company that then hired him to put the project on the rails. The new publication was in the field of international business and was addressed to high-level executives. For this reason it seemed to represent an interesting diversification for the company, which until then had published only quality periodicals for the general public. What Frank could not have known before joining the company was that his project had won out over another idea proposed to the president jointly by the circulation director and the executive editor. Everything went smoothly, however, at the start. His new colleagues were welcoming, and Frank was given a free hand in hiring and setting up the required new offices. He even heard that his president had cited his way of managing people as a good role model for other division heads. (Because he was pleased, Frank failed to see the danger in this.)

Some months into the project, little things began to go wrong. He could not get his dummies on time for distribution to advertising agencies. The chief accountant began criticising him about slight overspending in his budget. The circulation department claimed that it lacked the necessary experience in business publishing and insisted that a specialist be hired to help out. Thoroughly absorbed in his project, Frank failed to put the bits and pieces together. In any case, the magazine eventually appeared. Not only were the start-up costs high, but the number of subscribers fell short of expectations. The circulation department, of course, blamed the product rather than their marketing methods. Not surprisingly, advertisers took a wait-and-see attitude. As the problems accumulated Frank began to receive visits from the other department heads, who expressed concern about the viability of his project. Frank assured each of them that time would correct the situation. Of this he was absolutely confident until one evening, after work, the circulation director asked him to go for a drink in a nearby wine bar.

Her message was clear. Frank's project was costing all the top people in the organisation money in the form of reduced profit sharing. Throw in the towel now, she advised, or you'll be in real trouble. Three months later she was proved right. The president announced abruptly that he had sold the magazine (but not the personnel) to a publisher whose mission was 'more congruent' with that type of publication.

THE MORAL: **Selling your idea to the president is not enough if you haven't sold it to your colleagues as well.**

'I forgot to prepare my return'

John T saw his selection to run the German subsidiary of his sanitary supply company as a major breakthrough in his career. Before his departure he read up on the history and culture of Germany, and agonized over the language. Once on the spot in Düsseldorf, he settled quickly into his post as managing director. In the four years that followed he reorganised the subsidiary with the result that its market share rose from 18 to 24 per cent, with an equally satisfactory increase in net profit. John's main strength on his departure was in sales and marketing, but by the time of his return to London he could claim to be a well-rounded manager with proved abilities in finance and production management as well.

He was rewarded with the title of assistant general manager US (there were two others with the same title), an office, a secretary and no clear responsibilities. Instead of the open doors he had expected into the offices of his former colleagues at headquarters, he sensed that a distance had grown between them and him, that he was not really a part of any group. Even his access to his boss, the international vice-president, was limited because of the many preoccupations of the latter. There was an effort, all too obvious, to keep John busy – reorganisation of the company canteen, representation of the company at an international trade fair, attendance at various meetings. But these miscellaneous activities added up to nothing in terms of career progress. Little by little John came to feel more a stranger in his old environment than he ever had felt in the subsidiary. No one seemed interested in what was happening elsewhere in Europe, nor did he feel that there was any real recognition of his achievements there.

Within six months John found himself bored and disenchanted. He demanded a meeting with his vice-president during which it became clear that in reality there existed for him no open door to the future. In his absence, the jobs at headquarters at his level had been filled. While the vice-president assured John that he was welcome to continue doing sporadic tasks while waiting for something better, the message was clear that he might be happier elsewhere. A few days later John commenced a search of the job market.

What John did not realise is that his experience is all too frequently repeated in companies with international operations. Managements talk a lot about being world-minded, saying that the future lies in the development of foreign markets. It is ironic and a sad waste that the very people with successful experience abroad are likely to find the doors to the executive suite shut to them on their return. Colleagues tend to close ranks against people who have experienced, in their eyes, an uncomfortably high level of autonomy and responsibility. If, furthermore, they have really distinguished themselves in their foreign posts, they are an even greater threat and therefore a larger target for defensive action by the domestic contingent.

As John put it, he had been urged to study and prepare himself psychologically for the new experiences he was to face abroad. No one thought to mention that psychological preparation for the shock of returning home can be every bit as challenging as that of adapting to a foreign environment.

THE MORAL: **On your return from a successful campaign to build your company's affairs overseas expect no medals from management. Better instead to keep alert for opportunities elsewhere.**

'But that person was the perfect secretary'

That was the opinion Alan D had of Gilda before he was fired. As an account executive for a major advertising agency Alan kept in constant touch with the rumours that continually swirled about the agency business. One piece of gossip became so persistent that he felt it must have some basis in fact. This particular rumour had it that a larger agency was preparing to take over his company. As it happened, Alan was a graduate of the same university as the head of the agency named. Thinking it would do no harm to prepare his own future in case the takeover materialised, Alan wrote a handwritten note to his friend, suggesting that they meet one day for lunch. As a matter of routine he asked Gilda to make a photocopy to put in his personal file.

This was his mistake. Within a matter of hours, the chairperson of Alan's agency knew of the contact Alan was trying to establish. However, he never mentioned this fact. He simply called Alan into his office one Friday evening and announced that management had 'lost confidence' in him, and that his accounts were being reassigned to other account executives. He said, rather ominously, that he himself would explain the reasons for the change to the clients who would be affected.

Without any proof, without even a firm knowledge of the reason behind the chairperson's action, Alan had no ground for accusing Gilda of duplicity. It was only when he announced that he was leaving that he felt sure of her active role in the affair. She tried to appear surprised and uttered the right words of sympathy, but because a large part of Alan's business life had been spent studying human beings and their motivations, he saw through her. Yet he was also a realist and he decided to say nothing to Gilda. After all, the fact remained that she was an excellent secretary. And a loyal one, too, but obviously more devoted to the management upstairs than to her immediate boss.

THE MORAL: **Never confuse professional competence with personal loyalty.**

'I made a big splash'

Victor H was delighted with his new job as director of purchasing for a major company manufacturing a full line of security products for industry and for homes. One of the best features of his assignment, in his view, was the broad directive under which he was operating. His mission was to reduce the amount the company was paying for its purchases. Since the cost of materials and services represented 55 per cent of the company's expense, Victor saw an opportunity to make an important contribution to profit. Accustomed to working fast, he demanded competitive bids from suppliers, dropped some of them, added new ones and browbeat others into reducing their prices. Within a short while he was able to point to an overall reduction of purchasing costs of 2 per cent – an enormous saving in terms of money.

Victor's work was quickly recognised by his management and within three months he was awarded a significant increase in salary. Then the trouble began. His company's manufacturing was done in four separated subsidiaries, each devoted to a different product. The managers of these companies had long enjoyed autonomy in the matter of the purchases that were unique to their product lines. They also had 'friends' among the suppliers. Soon Victor's boss, the executive vice-president, began to receive telephone calls and memoranda from the local managers. The quality of such and such an item was not up to standard, they claimed; the delivery dates of other supplies were not respected; the after-sales service of certain suppliers was slow or non-existent. Soon the 'problems' were taking up an important percentage of the vice-president's time.

When the situation came to the attention of the president, he stated his wishes clearly. Investigate the validity of the complaints, he ordered his vice-president. If they were soundly based, go back to the former decentralised purchasing system, regardless of the cost. He did not have to add that such a move would, in effect, reduce Victor's job to a degree that would make his salary impossible to justify.

Fortunately the executive vice-president had a deep commitment to the new system since he himself had inaugurated it. He threw himself wholeheartedly into the investigation and finally came to the conclusion that 80 per cent of the complaints were largely unjustified. As for the others, he ordered Victor to work directly with the suppliers to eliminate the problems. This Victor was successful in doing and his new methods were adopted as permanent company policy.

However, Victor did not emerge entirely unscathed. He was criticised on the one hand by management for not having taken the time to 'sell' the local managers on the need for economy and, on the other hand, he faced constant guerrilla warfare with the bruised local managers. He now has the situation under control, but he understands today that his survival was a near thing.

THE MORAL: **No matter how bright you are, go into your new job with a low profile; scout out the opposition before acting if you are to avoid headaches later on.**

'I had nothing against them personally'

But Ralph W saw a chance to introduce some important savings into his company's operations. He had just been promoted to director of finance from his former post as chief accountant. For several months he had pointed out to his predecessor the high level of expenses in the sales department. The former holder of his post had always agreed with Ralph that 'something had to be done'. But for some reason there was no change. Not only did Ralph consider the sales department's entertainment and travel expenses to be out of line, but sometimes credit terms were extended without authorisation and even, in certain cases, discounts granted without consultation. It was true that sales were good and were growing, but Ralph felt it outrageous that budgets and procedures should be flouted with such impunity.

Now Ralph found himself at the same organisational level as Irwin, the commercial director. For the first time he felt he had the clout to take action and to make it stick. Recognising that his predecessor had got nowhere by talking, Ralph decided on a different tack. He instituted a weekly analysis of the situation and every Monday sent a memorandum to his president itemising the overspending in the sales department. A copy of each memo was sent to Irwin. In this manner, Ralph reasoned, he would have a cumulative written record in the hands of both the president and the sales manager. He was sure that action could not fail to be forthcoming. In this he was absolutely right.

However, the action unexpectedly originated from the president's office. He reported to Ralph that Irwin had come to him to give the required three months' notice of his departure from the company. His reasons were not clearly stated but the president was not without his intuitions.

'Those memos to sales.' he asked. 'Did you discuss with Irwin the points that you made?'

Ralph said he felt the figures spoke for themselves and said so.

'And Irwin didn't come to see you?'

'No.'

The president sighed. He pointed out that Irwin was the best sales manager in the business. Not only would his loss be sorely felt, but the thought that he might, if disaffected, go with a competitor turned the president's 'guts to water', as he dramatically put it. Then he talked about the differences between the mentality of a director of sales and the mentality of a financial officer – the one flexible, accustomed to talking things through; the other dispassionate, objective and tending to see reality in terms of what is clearly stated on paper. He pointed out, too, the chronic complaint of sales managers: 'While we sweat to bring in money, what is the contribution to revenues of the financial people who seem always to be trying to find ways to demotivate my salespeople?'

The president then arranged a three-way discussion of the situation between the two departments. There was a lot of heat generated in the meeting, but also some light. Ralph and Irwin finally agreed to hold regular interdepartmental sessions, with as many people involved from each department as might be needed to get to the bottom of whatever problems existed. With this decided, the president bowed out of the situation.

Three weeks later, Irwin mysteriously withdrew his resignation. It would be nice at this point to say that the problems between the two men were happily resolved forever after. Not surprisingly, the differences in their natures and their points of view continued. But each time the pressure rose dangerously high they let off steam and then reached some kind of resolution of the problem at hand. For both, but especially for Ralph, their rough passage proved, over a period of time, to be a growth experience in what amounted to a very special kind of interplanetary communication.

THE MORAL: **Memos are a dangerous substitute for face-to-face discussion of mutual problems.** QUESTION: **Does a really satisfactory substitute exist?**

Such examples of problems, and sometimes of solutions to problems, that can exist between colleagues could go on endlessly. However, without over-simplifying, we can see from the case studies above that the difficulties discussed came about because of different types of shortcomings on the part of the individuals involved. Among them are the following.

1 *A need for discretion* Papers that should be private are left about without sufficient thought to the consequences. Too much trust is placed in another person.
2 *Hubris* Excessive pride or self-confidence, the feeling that one can do no wrong. One result of this dangerous serendipity is a failure to listen to others – to discern their desires and motivations before acting. You may find that those others indeed have ways, sooner or later, of making their feelings clear.
3 *A predilection for written, rather than verbal, communication* How can we know their reaction at the moment a person receives a letter or memorandum? How can we mitigate a negative reaction without being present? Indeed such negative feelings are liable to fester and grow. This is not to say that the need for written communication does not often exist. That would be foolish. It is simply to state that face-to-face discussion should be favoured whenever it is appropriate.
4 *If you've sold a new project or idea to your boss, make sure your col-*

leagues are also convinced of its merits Otherwise their lack of enthusiasm may translate itself into something that might not be called sabotage, but that in terms of results may amount to much the same thing.

5 *If you accept an overseas assignment, don't expect a resounding welcome when you return to headquarters* Return with patience and discretion – or look elsewhere. Remember your potential to be either a threat or a bore – or both – to those colleagues who are already ensconced in the high-backed chairs.

PART 2: WORKING IN GROUPS

Some people find it amusing, some disconcerting, to observe eminent professors of business management locked in battle over the relative importance of teamwork versus 'bossism' to corporate success.

As for individual enterprises, large and small, traditional or pioneering, the truth of the matter is simply that what works works. It is demonstrable that certain companies can not only survive but thrive under heirarchial management, even under management-by-fear (if fuelled by recognised competence up top and by tangible rewards for good performance below). Others flourish in a group atmosphere of give and take, thesis and antithesis, that – when *it* works – produces a dynamic and simbiotic synthesis.

Despite the war of professional words, a two-pronged hypothesis is not hard to arrive at:

Element No. 1 – the success of Japanese industry has given business management in the developed countries a large shove toward circles of quality and other collective measures.

Element No. 2 – which is a basis, for example, of the viewpoint of Harold Bridger of the Tavistock Institute – top management today risks being overwhelmed by factors external to the day-to-day running of the company (concerns over environmental problems, community relations, technological breakthroughs, government interference). These and other distractions can result in a vacuum of direction in the middle management ranks. While their leaders are coping with matters emanating from the exterior, the key managers on the secondary level have two choices – each person can strive for a position of dominance over his collaborators or, in the overall interest of the group, opt for teamwork.

What follows is addressed to people who are more interested in assuring the success of their enterprise than in pulling off a successful power play. Perhaps like yourself, they consider their own well-being to be linked to the good overall health of the organisation. As a result they want to be effective collaborators, but almost always they find that this is not as easy as right thinking would like it to be.

What constitutes a good collaborator in a group setting? He or she is generally the person who recognises a fundamental fact. Ultimately, if the work of the group is to be successful, the personality of the group will not become the reflection of the personality of any single member. Instead the group will attain an identity of its own, completely apart from the identity of the individuals involved. Else it is not a functioning group.

This in no sense means that we must lose our own identity in the process of integrating into a group. In fact, the opposite is true. Only the person able to achieve a clear sense of his own unique individuality can identify with others of differing identities. This stands to reason. How can we recognise common feelings with others unless we are fully aware of, and able to identify, our own feelings?

Let us also accept then that group-work involves feelings every bit as much as it does brain-work. Until relatively recently the world of business has stressed the use of the 'head' almost to the elimination of the 'heart'. Even today a certain courage is required if one is to recognise, trust and to state aloud his own feelings.

The question arises: How can the members of a group equate the use of feelings with the need to reach rational consensus on matters that, after all, are intrinsically highly pragmatic? In seeking the answer to this question, you may find it useful first to study examples of how some typical individuals function within groups.

The profiles below are intended to provide you with a 'ready identification system' similar to the little silhouette cards carried by civilian aircraft spotters in the Second World War. You may well meet certain people you already have, or almost certainly will, encounter in group work. With this recognition, you should find it possible to monitor more effectively your own particular way of relating on a feeling level to each of them.

But here a word of warning is needed. Examples of the representative types I am going to describe below may not leap immediately to your mind. If it is true that teamwork is based in large part on feelings, it is also true that feelings are not always easy to recapture *after* the event. Therefore, I suggest that you stock into your inner bank of information these profiles. Then, in your work in groups, keep on the alert for the various types of behaviour depicted. Who knows, you may even recognise one or more of these tendencies to be a part of your own way of relating to others.

The professor

His or her way of functioning in groups is characterised by a tendency to seize upon some particular moment in a meeting to use as a springboard for a discourse that may be thoroughly tangential to the discussion at hand. If one or the other is available, he prefers to make use of a blackboard or a flip chart to illustrate his points – one, two, three, four and far beyond. The 'professor' tends to favour the general and the theoretical in his speech, leaving his auditors bored and with the uneasy feeling that no progress toward a decision is being made – unless, as is sometimes the case, another person present speaks up, saying 'I really don't see what Tom is driving at.' To voice such a thought obviously takes a bit of courage; the interrupter may be seen to confess that his intellectual stature is not up to following the close-knit, if far-from-the-point, arguments of the 'professor.'

Inside the professor

Why do some people prefer to make speeches rather than converse? Chances are, we are dealing here with a person who (1) has a highly structured way of thinking and (2) is by long habit accustomed to 'one-way' communication – from himself to others. His need for structure causes him real discomfort in group sessions where there is a flow of give and take and where people may say things that the Professor finds either not pertinent or even, in his view, rather stupid.

Because he is feeling a bit lost and uneasy, the Professor is likely to break in with the kind of communication that makes him most comfortable – that of a parent giving guidance. Certain personnel managers, human relations directors and directors of security fall easily into the 'professorial' role. On the one hand, they may have the habit of categorising people into grades, ranks and salary brackets – all a part of their structured environment; on the other hand, they see the great bulk of personnel as dependents and therefore in need of counselling. (Let me say that in no way do I question the warmth or goodwill of such professorial types. I am simply saying that they do not always facilitate group work.)

How to deal with the Professor when he is in full flight? I have already suggested that one way is to interrupt him with a confession that you are not grasping the point of his lecture and how it applies to the situation at hand. This carries an obvious danger that the Professor may, in fact, redouble his words in an effort to shoe-horn his message into the context of the group discussion. Sometimes, therefore, shock treatment remains the only answer: 'I can't help but ask if anyone other than myself is feeling a bit bored with this line of discussion.' Certain eyebrows will shoot up but you may also reap a certain number of amens. In any case, don't be surprised if the Professor has gone, suddenly and blessedly, mute.

The auditor

In many meetings, we find a person who is silent, not out of timidity but because he or she is absorbing the pros and cons of each statement by the other members of the group. Indeed his silence sometimes causes a certain discomfort around the table because no one is quite certain whether or not in spirit he is inside the group or outside. Like a poker player he waits to declare his hand. And, like a financial auditor, any remarks he does make will tend to be critical, identifying the flaws in the statements of others but rarely contributing creatively. The label 'auditor' can in some situations be more specific than I intended, for this person may indeed come from the financial department of the company.

Inside the auditor
Two qualities mark the mentality that I arbitrarily call the mentality of the auditor. First is his habit of focusing on past performance – consequently, in group work, after digesting what the others have been saying, he tries from time to time to extrapolate conclusions from the discussion; the second characteristic is that he often is a pessimist. Putting these two tendencies together, we find ourself in the presence of a person who sees his role in the group to be that of a critic and a processor of information. Useful as this role is, he at the same time has difficulty fitting that information constructively into a positive or creative context. This may explain his silence leading up to the point where he feels he has stored sufficient data to enable him to make a judgement. Then, as we have pointed out, his judgements are likely to be negative – like the 'notes' found at the end of a company audit.

The Auditor's role, while more backward than forward looking, is a useful one in the sense that his objectivity may provide benchmarks for occasional stock-taking as to the progress of the discussion. 'Where have we been'? 'Where are we now'? 'Where do we seem to be going'? These are questions essential to group work if the objectives of the meeting are not to be lost from sight.

The Auditor turns out to be one of the easiest to integrate into group sessions. Once he has spoken his piece, rationally as ever, the moment has come for comment by the other members of the group. Only one response makes sense: 'It seems clear that you do not approve of the proceedings up to now. Granted, your points are well taken, but would you please share with us your ideas of a more constructive approach.' More likely than not, the answer will be along these lines: 'At the moment I have not formulated a specific plan of action. Since this is a subject that obviously requires study and thought, I'll be planning to give you my views at our next session.'

The take-charge guy

The meeting has hardly opened when this person speaks up. He or she wants to set parameters for the discussion, to have a clearly organised agenda, to define objectives. If others protest that talking about what they are going to talk about is likely to hamper ideas and decision-making, the take-charge guy will speak about the need for 'some discipline' in order to avoid 'wasting time.' If the conversation then swirls out of his control, he may well lapse into silence, having lost his bearings.

Inside the take-charge guy

Whereas the Professor aims to have the attention of the group focused on himself, the Take-Charge Guy wants to control the proceedings. In spirit, he belongs to pre-war management, which viewed its role through the prism of the hierarchy: 'Someone has to be in charge here and it might just as well be me.' Some people see this kind of reflex as the sign of a 'natural leader'. More accurate would be to say that he has the habits of a 'natural boss'. Behind this person's drive to impose agendas and parameters on the others may well lurk a suspicion that the group could control him if he fails to control the group. In other words, he might have to give up the security blanket of authority for the collective will of the group.

The Take-Charge Guy may not be as great a threat to group functioning as would appear from his grab for control. To oppose him directly is likely to be counter-productive, simply increasing the flow of his combative hormones (with which he is probably well supplied). More productively, you might abruptly bring up for discussion a really substantive point that has nothing to do with arranging forms and procedures. The rest of the group may well take the bait, leaving the Take-Charge Guy with two choices, either to insist on sticking to his fixation on setting 'parameters', or to catch up with the group as the discussion moves along to more important matters. Chances are, he will opt for the second alternative.

The introvert

Shyness among adults is far more common than most of us admit. Probably the reason for this lack of recognition is the fact that timidity is somehow often equated with weakness. This may also be the reason why human beings have invented so many ways of concealing shyness, from bombastic behaviour to constant joking. But here we are speaking of people who do not make use of such defences – who tend to be retiring and even sometimes seem unsure of themselves. They may well be the younger and less experienced members of the group. In meetings they may try to speak up, but often they wait that extra second before doing so and as a result they lose the floor to someone else. More likely than not they fail to speak with conviction once they are heard. Yet such diffident people often are precisely the ones who have most thoroughly reflected on a problem, seeing it from numerous angles that may escape the more egregious types around the table.

Inside the introvert

Certain people are relatively at ease in one-to-one contacts but stiff and awkward in group meetings. Dealing with a single person, they find the signals relatively clear. In such situations, they are dealing with a limited spectrum of verbal and non-verbal signals. In groups, it is different. The signals are multiple and mixed and the words may tumble forth from various mouths, communicating a potpourri of ways of thinking and feeling. In such situations, a retiring junior may be seen as a non-contributor to the work of the group. If this judgement is correct, the fault may in fact lie more with the others than with the individual himself.

Because the Introvert's thoughts and feelings probably are dense and complex and because he is ill at ease when the talk darts from one person (one personality, that is) to another, he may not enter spontaneously into a situation of give-and-take. Here you have a splendid opportunity to advance the work of the group. Rather than to allow the Introvert to find himself excluded from the group, be sure to look in his direction from time to time. Listen as well. If he tries by signal or verbally to enter into the discussion, you can help him by declaring, 'I think Jim has been trying to make a point. How about giving him a chance?' Most people, having ignored Jim, will not have noticed his efforts to be heard but once he does speak up, he may well have something useful to say.

May I add that you will win a friend and future supporter in assuring Jim's contribution to the proceedings.

The bomb-thrower

This person needs attention and he or she knows how to get it. In a group effort he likes to put the 'cat among the pigeons' by making proposals that verge on the outrageous but which have the merit of a certain off-beat logic. ('Why don't we just set fire to the warehouse and collect the insurance?') The result is indignation among those present and a glorious hubbub of attack and counter-attack. By the time calm is restored the group unhappily realises that the time spent putting him down has represented a period of no progress.

Inside the bomb-thrower

If an election were held for the least popular member of most groups, the Bomb-Thrower would probably win by a landslide. He sometimes throws his bombs with a suppressed grin, signalling that he is perpetrating mischief, thus making his manner even less appreciated by others. And yet … and yet … he certainly is a stimulating (to put it mildly!) presence and he sometimes forces his colleagues to step outside the immediate problem and to take a fresh look at the situation.

'There's no reason for our offices to be in such a high-rent area. Let's sell the building, rake in a profit and move the outfit to the suburbs.' The Bomb-Thrower knows the prestige value of the present address and he also knows full well that the top brass would resist violently such a drastic change in their living–working habits. And yet, at the same time, there is a certain sense in what he is saying. If that were not the case, he would simply be told off by the other members of the group. However, he has thrown them a bone with some meat on it and now he can sit back and enjoy the commotion while the others attack it and himself – and sometimes each other.

You can recognise the Bomb-Thrower's game with a little practice. The clue is in his apparent enjoyment of the proceedings. He may, in fact, be the only person uninterested in his proposals. However, he will occasionally fling a little fuel onto the fire by defending his position with a certain vigour. And that is the sum of his real participation.

What is really going on here? The chances are that the Bomb-

Thrower is a deeply divided person. He wants and needs to be the centre of attention but he lacks the belief that he can succeed by means of a classic give-and-take. Like an old-fashioned anarchist, he throws his bomb and in the ensuing bruhaha silently slips away.

How are you going to put an end to the Bomb-Thrower's game? In this particular case you might consider direct confrontation. Right after he throws the next bomb and before the hue and cry starts up, ask a pointed question: 'Just what is going on here? Is this a serious proposition? If so, tell us how it applies to our discussion. Or are you by any chance using the group for your own amusement? In that case, I'm sure the others would be as unhappy as I am.'

Call his bluff and you defuse both the bomber and his bombs.

The note-taker

We all know people who are so addicted to taking notes that they (1) are always a little behind what is being said and (2) are unable to observe the all-important non-verbal signals by which others reveal, often in spite of themselves, their feelings of boredom or enthusiasm, assent or dissent. In his concentration on pen and paper, the Note-Taker risks flying blind as he substitutes the mechanics of writing for the engagement of his feelings.

Inside the note-taker

The compulsive note-taker probably is a person not wholly at ease with the spoken word because of its way of mixing feelings with fact. Possibly having an engineering or technical background, he tells himself that he will need copious notes for study later on. In actual fact, he is intent on reducing the intangible to the tangible where he feels most comfortable. Unfortunately, one effect of his scurrying pen may be that he is missing an essential part of group activity – the part having to do with everything that falls between the lines of his notes.

I recall one Note-Taker's sudden recognition of the degree to which he had become detached from the group. Someone had just voiced his unhappiness with the way the discussion had been tending for the past ten minutes. 'Pointless,' was the way he put it. The Note-Taker at this point slapped down his pen. 'Fantastic,' he said, 'that is exactly the word I have just written down.' In other words, he had disposed of his feelings by committing them to paper rather than by sharing them, as the other person had done.

You can help bring the Note-Taker into the group. Catch him when he is at his most industrious by shooting a direct question to him. He may look up in some confusion, embarrassed at having missed the last words of the discussion. He might even ask to have them repeated. Administer the treatment from time to time. He will get the point – that more important communications were under way than the communication he was having between himself and his pad of paper.

The peace-maker

To seem to be critical of someone who is earnestly trying to make peace is a thankless, even hazardous position. Here we have a person who sees some merit in nearly every proposition. If dissent begins to become spirited he will point out the nugget of truth that lay hidden behind what was simply, perhaps, an unfortunate manner of presentation. Should the argument flair into anger, he is there to pour oil on the turbulent waters by suggesting that, after all, Tom's remark was made in good faith and that he was speaking for the collective well-being of the organisation.

Inside the peace-maker

If you look into the past of the Peace-Maker, you might find that his or her early years were marked by quarrels and perhaps, even, a divorce or separation between parents. In such a situation, a child is bound to feel panic. After all, those early family disputes threatened not only his security but his whole world. He may have tried – probably unsuccessfully – to act as peacemaker between his father and mother. Now, as an adult, he perceives conflict to be loaded with danger, a threat to be headed off or covered up wherever possible.

The Peace-Maker thus is the mirror-image of the Bomb-Thrower who delights in havoc. The Peace-Maker will try to mediate between warring camps or individuals, explaining one to the other, modifying and mollifying. Whereas the Bomber likes to throw oil on the fire, the Peace-Maker pours it on troubled waters. He feels, sometimes correctly, that he is performing a service by preventing matters from 'getting out of hand'. But there exists for him a further source of satisfaction; he assumes that he has won admiration as a result of his concern for the cohesion of the group.

Sadly, we must face the fact that the Peace-Maker is not an entirely constructive element. Glossing over differences, perhaps making people regret their spontaneity, can work against a group effort. The differences will remain and along with them a lurking conviction that they really should have been ventilated. Essentially, what the Peace-Maker is conveying is a lack of confidence in the efficacy of frank and open group activity.

I feel that this person merits particular attention. At such times when you perceive that the group is quite content to bury a real division thanks to the Peace-Maker's balm, I suggest you intervene. 'Have we really worked through this question? What is the consensus of the group of this point?' Innocent questions, but perhaps useful.

Conflicts avoided are not conflicts resolved. They will surely break out again – in some other form, at some other time, unless someone respects their utility. Perhaps that person is yourself.

The star

The man of charisma – and one who knows it – is another threat to productive group activity. He seems often to be there to play the star – to purse his lips in thought, to gesticulate dramatically in making his points, to use his voice not only as an organ of persuasion but sometimes to over-ride others in mid-sentence. This is not to deny the value of charm and forcefulness; they can make even the dullest subject come to life. But at the same time, the other members of the group may well be asking themselves whether the Star sees their role is that of collaborators or claque.

Inside the star

How do we deal with the person who takes over a group session, not by openly seeking control but simply by force of personality? He knows the arts of seduction and he knows how to sell himself and his ideas. He may even at first come across as a rather modest chap, eager to hear the views of others. Little by little, however, the attention of the group becomes focused on this person – or should I say, personage? There is an increasing danger that he will dominate the meeting and that the group will cease to be a unity but rather a collection of satellites orbiting about one individual.

The person in the role of the Star may very well be someone who has attained a position higher than the other members of the group. To his natural authority is thus added the weight of the post he holds. Accustomed to authority, he may come on softly but none the less the others are fully aware of his potency. How can one deal with this kind of magnetism in order to protect the integrity of the group? Or should you even try to deal with him? (The possibility of retribution later, outside the group, looms as only too real!) I suggest that there is only one clear course of action. This is to ask questions. They should be very specific questions, having to do with details of some general subject under discussion. If you pose them in a true spirit of

inquiry – not in a needling fashion – you could be pleasantly surprised by the result. The Star may reflect a moment and then say, 'I
don't feel I have all the facts needed to answer your question. On the
other hand, Jim here is something of a specialist in the matter. Why
don't we hear from him?'

The Star very likely did not get to be a star simply because of his
personality. Behind the façade, there is probably a serious person,
concerned as much with substance as with form. It may not, in fact,
even be his intention to dominate the group. That he does so is, let
us say, his karma. When you bring him face to face with specifics,
you are not an aggressor. He well knows that the facts are important;
you stand a good chance not only of winning his respect, but that of
the group for nudging the discussion towards solid ground.

The sycophant

We can talk as much as we like about the desirability of equality in
groups, but almost always there is present a person who is 'more
equal than the others.' This may be due to his title or to his age or to
his reputation for accomplishment. But whatever the source of this
super-equality, the Sycophant will be drawn to him like a bee to a
dewy rose. The Sycophant will agree, he will constantly seek eye contact with the super-equal, and he will oppose with vigour anyone who
differs with the postulations of the object of his admiration (and/or
ambition). In other words, his contribution is no longer to the work of
the group but rather to the nourishment of the ego of the dominant
person.

Inside the sycophant

Unless the sycophant is extremely clever, he is not likely to win the
affection of the group. His focus, in fact, is more one that might later
take place outside the room than on the business at hand. His support, his questions and his affirmative signals tend to be directed
toward the person he had identified as the most influential. Unlike
the others, most of whom are interested in the substance of the discussion, he is intent on scoring points for himself.

Dealing with this person is not easy. Good sense dictates that any
effort to confront the situation head-on is likely to be counter-productive, not only destabilising the Sycophant but also earning,
perhaps, the ill will of the object of his admiration. Frankness must
have its limits, even in group work!

There is another way. Most parents know that children can often
be diverted by a change of subject. Rather than to permit the Syco-

phant to carry on a dialogue with the target of his ambitions, I suggest you fire at him a direct question on some matter of substance, preferably a question representing a radical change of subject. While he wrestles with his reply, he cannot continue to focus on his target.

Of course, the admired one himself may be equally conscious of what has been going on. Indeed, it would be a mistake to assume a lack of awareness on his part. For him to reorient the discussion toward another person or persons is a relatively simple matter. In other words, let's hope that he will deal with the matter instead of yourself.

The facilitator

Up to this point we have been describing various kinds of behaviour in groups. They all have one quality in common. Each individual discussed seems to be as preoccupied with what the group can do for him as he is with facilitating the work of the group. The Facilitator, on the other hand, fills the role of catalyst. He understands and accepts his own identity and this enables him to relate his feelings to the feelings of others. Thus in a group he often voices thoughts that the others have but for various reasons do not vocalise. So doing, he sometimes strikes a common chord that enables the group to get on with its work. In pulling together the group, while at the same time respecting the individuality of each of its members, he is able to help bring into focus diverse ideas and personalities.

The Facilitator, however, differs in one important respect from a catalyst. Whereas the composition of a catalyst is unchanging, this is not his case. Since he himself is very much a part of the action, his ideas might well be modified by what he hears from other members of the group. Often, indeed, this is what happens. If not, he would not be a working part of the group.

Inside the facilitator

Somewhere inside the Facilitator we will probably find elements of all of the other profiles described here. This is what gives him the ability to empathise with the disparate natures present in the group. Because the Facilitator is not particularly interested in ascendancy, he avoids the danger of becoming a target for the competitiveness of the others. Thus he is able to get on with his work of facilitation.

In connection with each of the foregoing profiles, I have suggested ways to bring people into the group process despite any tendency to be self-serving. This turns out, in fact, to be the objective of the Facilitator even though he might not be consciously aware of his mission.

The suggestions I have made are typical of the way he might go about doing his work of integration. However, what I have not stressed is that the work is hard. On the one hand the Facilitator must be following in detail the flow of the discussion while on the other he is constantly tuned in to what is happening on the all-important feeling level. Not only is the job demanding; it also calls for courage of a special kind – the courage sometimes to say things that others are thinking but are unwilling to give voice to.

However, the Facilitator has his compensation as the group comes together and begins to emerge with its own identity entirely separate from the identity of the individual members – including his own. He knows that this is in no way his own personal handiwork. He realises that somewhere within everyone there lies some of the qualities that belong to the Facilitator. He senses also that it is the release of these qualities that makes successful group work possible.

You may have noted that in none of the profiles discussed have I used the label 'Leader'.

This is because in group work the true leader can be none other than the person I have described last – the Facilitator.

CHAPTER 18
Relations with subordinates

Up to now in Part II of this book we have focused on two major aspects of career advancement: upward mobility within a hierarchy and the quest for lateral synergy in our relations with our colleagues. The third dimension – relations with subordinates – is of equal importance because, first, the overall results you show are often linked to the quality of the work produced by the people under your authority, and secondly, the support or lack of support these people give you within your organisation can have a marked influence on your career progression.

It is important to realise a basic premise underlying what is to follow. This is the fact that we are once again in the position of discussing hierarchical 'over–under' relationships. We should admit that very few, if any, businesses have so far reached the point where all management functions can be handled through group activity. Probably most never will attain this Nirvana of the socio-psychologists.

Rigid rules and generalisations about how to treat your subordinates are liable to be more frustrating than helpful. A large part of leadership is purely a matter of instinct. An approach that may work well for one superior can prove hopeless to another. Take, for example, the matter of charisma – a word we have used once or twice before. For the person with a really magnetic personality, charisma can be the motor that lifts a team from a mediocre to an excellent performance. For the individual who lacks this quality there are, none the less, other means to motivate people – among them, showing genuine interest in their work, giving them feedback and encouragement, and manifesting concern for their growth and progression. In other words, there is obviously room for many different types of leadership; it is, after all, the result that counts. Each of us must learn – often by trial and error – which aspects of our personality can most usefully be harnessed to the activity of leading others.

Apart from the matter of making the best use of our personalities, there is the all-important question of the kind of context in which we are functioning. The two must be in harmony. A compatibility between our nature and the type of work we do is essential if we are to be 'in sync' with our subordinates. For example, it is obvious that the leadership roles of a director of research and of a director of sales are radically different – so different that it is impossible to imagine a reversal of roles. These two examples, which I have chosen at random, are revealing because they speak on the one hand of a staff (or functional) position and on the other hand of a line (or operational) responsibility.

At this point I should be clear on how I use the words line and staff. Whether or not you agree with my definition is unimportant. What is important is to avoid confusion as we proceed to discuss these two basic work contexts. I see the line manager as a person who directly 'makes things happen', a person who has their hands on the levers that control the functioning of a department or the entire enterprise. Conversely, the staff person's responsibility is to provide the line managers with the ingredients that make possible their management activities – information of all sorts, including financial, research results, long-range forecasts, marketing surveys, legal advice and consultancy.

Among the individuals I have counselled I can think of two types who are particularly uncomfortable in their roles. One is the person who has passed from a line to a staff function. The other is the individual who has switched from a staff to a line job. For the first person, the absence of direct and visible results of their efforts is as painful as the changed quality of the leadership function. In the case of the reverse change, the staff person finds a line role a source of stress and anxiety – totally apart from their nature and experience. The staff person comes to realise that at heart they are not a mover and shaker, and that a more cerebral activity, for example, is what really gives satisfaction.

The difference in the two mentalities required to carry out line and staff functions successfully is apparent. However, the world of work is far too complex to be reduced to such black and white categories. Probably no job is 100 per cent line or 100 per cent staff. The sales manager certainly has some 'staffy' work to do – preparation of budgets and forecasts, analysis of field reports, approval of expense accounts etc. On the other hand, there is a line element implicit in the vast majority of staff jobs. The research director can have very important responsibilities in many companies, such as pharmaceuticals, household products and electronics.

If you are to be in a post that makes the fullest possible use of your character and personality, you are well advised to analyse your characteristics, and compare them with the characteristics of people who are successful in staff and line positions. However, it is not enough for you, after reflection, simply to decide 'I am a staff person' or 'I am a line manager'. Since everyone is, to some degree, a mixture of these qualities, more precision is needed. In other words you need to find out the answer to the question: 'To what extent am I "staff" and to what extent am I "line"?'

The questions that follow are intended to help you sort out various qualities within yourself and so to measure, with some degree of accuracy, the relative importance of these two aspects of your professional profile.

A MODEL LINE MANAGER

There follows a list of qualities that I have identified as belonging to that very rare person who is by nature 100 per cent operational. Beside each characteristic, give yourself a rating from a minimum of 1 if the description in no way fits you to a maximum of 5 if you feel you correspond fully to the description.

The line manager:

welcomes responsibility enthusiastically   _____

is basically optimistic by nature   _____

can, when necessary, make quick, intuitive decisions   _____

knows the arts of politics and manipulation   _____

is creative and innovative, and likes new ideas   _____

seeks variety and challenge   _____

reads widely and has a thirst for information   _____

has a good command of both figures and words   _____

can motivate a team and is a natural leader   _____

can be very tough when required   _____

has good health and a very high energy level   _____

is good on their feet, addressing groups   _____

puts business life before family life   _____

is more oriented towards the sources of power
than downwards   _____

adapts quickly to new situations   _____

takes a long-term view of the future   _____

Total possible score: 80   **Your score:**   _____

A MODEL STAFF PERSON

Few persons are 100 per cent staff oriented. Listed below are the characteristics most commonly found among staff people. Compare yourself, description by description with each of these statements and give yourself a score, 1 to 5, to indicate the degree to which you resemble each description.

The staff person:

strives for perfection in the job at hand   _____

visualises problems more readily than opportunities   _____

tolerates routine rather well when necessary   _____

prefers regularity in working hours   _____

shuns 'small talk'   _____

seeks equilibrium between business and family life   _____

puts family well-being ahead of career   _____

is more at ease with concepts and intangibles than with
people   _____

has strong analytical abilities   _____

is more at ease with subordinates than superiors   _____

actively defends subordinates who are attacked by
superiors   _____

is detail minded   _____

delegates to subordinates with difficulty   _____

tends to be pessimistic   _____ always studies carefully before making decisions   _____

prefers security to risk   _____

Total possible score: 80   **Your score:**   _____

WHAT IS YOUR IDENTITY?

I have already expressed my distrust of 'scores' applied to the marvellous and subtle qualities that constitute any human being. However, here it is not the total of an absolute score that is meaningful. It is the relative balance between your line and staff qualities that is indicative.

Suppose, to take an easy example, that you scored 40 points out of 80 in terms of your correspondence with the line manager's profile and 40 out of 80 as concerns your relative fitness for a staff position. In this case the conclusion is apparent: you are likely to be most effective in a post that demands, in as equal a measure as possible, these two types of qualities (for example, a director of finance).

If, to take another example, your score for line management is 60, whereas your score in a staff role is 20, you are well advised to seek a post which has plenty of responsibility. On the other hand, if the two scores are reversed, it is obvious that a staff role is going to be the one that will bring you the most satisfaction and growth.

'AM I IN THE RIGHT ROLE?'

The role of line manager

If your scores indicate that your line quotient is extremely high and staff quotient low, typical posts, among others, in which you are likely to be the most effective could be as follows (depending, of course, on your age and career progress).

(*Note:* Job titles are hard to define since the content of a post can vary within the framework of each title. However, the intention here is to view each title in its most classic and generally accepted sense.)

President
   Executive vice-president
   Director, division
General manager
   Assistant general manager
   Commercial director
   Director of sales
   Regional sales manager
   Director of agency (bank or broker)
   Advertising manager
Industrial director
   Production manager
   Plant manager
   Factory manager
   Materials handling manager
Project manager
Controller

The staff manager's role

If your score reveals that you possess a more or less equal mixture of staff and line characteristics you are likely to find most satisfaction in posts that are 'line within staff', meaning that the role of the group as a whole is a support role to management, but that the direction of the group demands strong qualities of leadership. Among such positions are the following.

Company secretary
   Director of human relations
   Personnel manager
   Head of recruitment
Technical director
   Manager, management information systems
   Manager, electronic data processing
Director of research, production
Director of research, laboratory
Director of research, applications
Director of research, marketing
Chief accountant
   Internal audit manager
Group product manager
   Product manager

Purchasing director
Logistics manager
Publications director
Export manager

The predominantly staff role

If your score is heavily weighted towards a staff role as being the optimum environment for you, you would be most efficient in one of the following posts.

Assistant to:
    President
    Executive vice-president
Internal auditor
Treasurer
    Foreign exchange officer
Chief of long-range planning
    Chief economist
    Macro-economist
    Economist
Public relations director
    In charge, financial public relations
Internal consultant
Head of organisation and methods
Head of quality control
Researcher
Safety engineer
Stockholders' representative (board member of subsidiaries)
Head of legal department
    Staff lawyer
Company ombudsman
Commodity trader
Sales engineer

LEADERSHIP IN THE THREE ROLES

The line manager

The way up for most line managers is fraught with pitfalls. You enter your company well endowed with intelligence and energy – and ambition. As a result of this trio of qualities it usually is not long before you begin to get visible results of your efforts in the form of successes that attract the attention not only of management but of your colleagues. Then you notice that one of the underlying motives of some people is one that is foreign to you – jealousy. A further step in the learning process is to come to understand that jealous people do not always compete solely with the weapons of industry and technical competence, but also with what might be called Factor X. This is the factor that Machiavelli examined in *The Prince*. Earlier we discussed some of the methods that certain people use to manipulate other people. One conclusion emerges clearly from a study of the various ways 'office politicians' operate: the person who rises up the ladder of top management cannot remain a sentimentalist for long – if indeed they ever were.

In other words you have to toughen up in the course of playing the office version of the game 'king of the castle'. As a result the problem of the true line manager is more often to soften your approach rather than to exercise your natural authority freely. Having found out on your way up that certain good subordinates react negatively to overt displays of power, you have to learn to hold back when you see that a more reasoned approach is the best way of producing the results you seek. However, do not spurn the use of fear as a motivator in certain situations and with certain people. While usually scorning academic or laboratory psychology, most successful line managers are very able psychologists in practice.

As pointed out earlier, an ambitious line manager never neglects relations with those in power above them. Except when we are in business for ourselves, we always have to deal with a source of authority – whether it is a general manager, a president, a chairperson or, ultimately, a board of directors representing a more or less amorphous group of stockholders. You may wish to maintain an 'open door' policy towards the people to whom you report, but there are periods when it is impossible to make time for everyone.

Indeed, the optimum utilisation of your time is often a question that preoccupies you. In this connection, you may have absorbed one of the lessons of the anthropologists who have traced back to prehistoric times the fact that a group of 10 to 12 individuals is the optimum size of a hunting group under a single leadership. Remember the 12 apostles? It is interesting to note how many boards and other working groups are still about this size. To try to deal directly with a greater number is to risk a loss of control because of the demands on your time. To keep in direct contact with fewer people presents the opposite risk of finding yourself cut off from what is going on in your organisation.

Sooner or later every line manager has to come face to face with questions that loosely group themselves under the heading of 'morality'. I am not speaking here of dramatic lapses from proper behaviour, such as misuse of funds or the acceptance of financial and other 'favours'. The questions are likely to be more subtle than that. Do you reveal that someone competing with you for promotion has a drinking problem? Do you deal openly and frankly in situations where – as in poker – it is better not to reveal your hand? During a strike do you supply a big and profitable customer from existing stocks at the expense of the smaller, struggling client? One of the quandaries faced by line managers as they move upwards in their organisation is how to square the realities of a fiercely competitive business culture with the rules of morality with which we have often been inculcated throughout our childhood and youth.

Among the most troublesome questions is that of how to be a good family person and still perform successfully in the super-heated, stressful environment of modern business. Sooner or later it becomes clear that there are no black-and-white answers – that compromises are to be made – or else you will have to elect to drop out of the line of authority to seek a more staff-oriented position. Every person has to find the answers for themselves. However, one consequence is likely to be pain, since the rules of the game of business are frequently not in accord with the most idealistic rules of personal behaviour. To find the right balance is simply one more challenge – or burden – that adds to a need among top line managers to have a very robust constitution.

But the human relations skills required of a line manager are only a part of your required equipment. You must also keep on feeding your personal, interior bank of information. If yours is a technical environment, especially in the field of electronics or bio-genetics, simply keeping up with the state of the art is a formidable challenge. At the same time, a person who wishes to maintain a human, non-technical contact with subordinates, peers and superiors has an obligation to read widely and to absorb a variety of information on the state of the world – its trends in the sciences, in the arts, and in politics and international relations. To neglect this kind of internal nourishment with information of all sorts from the outside is likely to stop you developing. And development is the key to a person moving into a leadership role. It enables you to perceive new horizons; it helps you to maintain contact with other thinking people and it is a constantly renewing source of creativity.

Finally, the line manager of the present or of the future must sooner or later face up to the question of what you are seeking from other people – in bald terms, whether it is their love or their respect. Here it is possible to be categorical. If you are a line manager whose priority it is to satisfy through your subordinates and/or your colleagues a craving for affection you are well advised to face up to that fact and then to recognise at the earliest possible opportunity that you are on a slippery slope. Objectively you know how easy it is to be fooled by people who understand this need that so many superiors have. Subjectively the view is different. Loneliness is part and parcel of leadership. Thus, from subordinates a word of understanding here, an expression of admiration there, an offer of support on another occasion – all of these can make their mark in the soft underbelly of the executive psyche.

If this is a danger – and it should be recognised as such – then you are well advised to keep in mind one thought: more bosses have been victimised by supposedly loyal supporters than by less loyal staff. On the other hand, consider the situations where a leader has taken a firm stand and has rigorously pursued, even perhaps bru-tally, the path they have chosen as the correct one. On the way the leader collects enemies and is perhaps criticised as being headstrong and insensitive to others. But finally, if the leader has produced results, they find – perhaps to their surprise – that the leader is revered – a step beyond love. Along with the material gains resulting from the leader's contributions, this should provide most reasonable human beings with a satisfactory amount of appreciation.

Remember, in comparing yourself with this profile of a hypothetical '100 per cent' line manager, that the characteristics described will seldom apply fully to any particular individual. What is important is the degree to which you deviate from this portrait. If the deviation is large, you will be more likely to find yourself in the domain of staff functions, the subject of our next discussion.

The staff manager

Here we are speaking of the person who has important line responsibilities for a group of some size that is engaged in a functional activity such as accounting. What I have said above about the 100 per cent line manager applies to a greater or lesser extent here, depending on the size of the staff manager's responsibility in terms of numbers of people and in terms of the autonomy granted by management. If the scale of responsibility is modest the description that follows of 'the staff person' is likely to be more applicable.

As a result of the fact that the staff manager's role is part line and part staff, you are invited to determine for yourself to what extent in your particular situation the foregoing description of the line manager and to what extent the following discussion of the purely staff person will apply.

The staff person

Many of the problems of management that are a part of the everyday life of a line manager simply do not exist for the staff person. In the first place, the number of people for whom you are responsible is likely to be limited – from one (a secretary perhaps) to several dozen in the case of a large research department. In the second place there is a homogeneity of interest within the group. The members are likely to share with you the primary goal which is, quite clearly, to produce an excellent product or service, as the case might be. In addition, the very content of the work contributes to mutual understanding; a researcher can understand without difficulty the set of mind of another researcher, just as economists can relate to other economists and accountants to accountants. This is very different from the many types of groups a top line manager must somehow pull together – engineers who have to coordinate with sales types, advertising people with financial controllers, factory managers with marketing people.

We must not go too far in simplifying the description of the professional life of a staff person. There is indeed another side to the picture. It centres on the fact that staff work is often hard to quantify and therefore difficult to assess in terms of added value to the organisation. In pharmaceutical research, for example, enormous amounts of time, talent and money can be expended before a breakthrough is achieved. In an activity of long-range planning, the accuracy or otherwise of the staff person's forecasts may not be fully known within a decade. This lack of a means to measure contribution creates one of the chief problems faced by staffers. Automatically, in the absence of objective measurements, other criteria flow into the vacuum. The criteria to which I refer group themselves around the talent, or lack of talent, that each person possesses in their ability to 'sell themselves' inside their organisation.

One of the purest forms of non-line activity is that of lecturer in a university or advanced institute of learning such as a business school. Lecturers have no subordinates and the real measure of the success of their efforts lies often with their students rather than in any objective evaluation by the school authorities. Since their popularity in the classroom is as likely to arouse jealousy as admiration, academics possess only two other ways to demonstrate their effectiveness objectively – through the results of research or by way of published works. This leaves open a third and less objective approach which means, in simple terms, finding ways of gaining the approval of the people who count most in the management of the organisation. For this reason, campus political infighting – contrasting as it does with the stereotyped public image of the serene academic world – has become the subject of numerous books and plays.

To a greater or lesser extent the same considerations apply to staff people in the world of business. The difference is that, in many cases, the staff role in business most often carries with it a responsibility for a certain number of subordinates. Moreover, it is often the relationships with like-minded people in the group that provide the staff person with a major source of satisfaction. However, in nurturing their people, helping them to grow and in being readily available to them, many staff supervisors develop a biased kind of loyalty – downwards rather than towards the management of the enterprise.

In defending 'their people' against attack, staff people may find themselves unwittingly in positions of resistance against the very sources of power that can ensure their future progress. Their downward orientation can at the same time expose them to other potential dangers. Often their interest in the details of the work the subordinates are doing can mean that staff people are poor delegators, afflicted with a lamentable itch to intervene in the tasks that can and should be carried out by their people. This predilection for detail and perfectionism can not only irritate the juniors but at the same time can divert the staff person's attention away from what is going on in the rest of the organisation. They may be astonished to find themselves overlooked at the end of the year when salary increases and promotions are passed out by management.

Whether we are speaking of 'line' or 'staff' the conclusion is always the same: the attention to human relations, particularly upwards towards the source of power, is essential, not only for career progression but even in terms of security of employment. In either case, the person who relies wholly on their abilities, energy and moral qualities may, unfortunately, be overlooking the fourth dimension, the quality of their communications, affective as well as intellectual.

CHAPTER 19

When goodbye is the best answer

Before the Second World War an individual who stayed with a single employer for 20 years was admired for stability and loyalty.

Today a person whose résumé shows that kind of longevity of employment is regarded with scepticism. Professional recruiters will wonder about the lack of variety in the person's experience. They will also question their initiative and readiness to adapt to new situations.

In other words, there once was a time when a person married their company 'for better or for worse', but in any case for the entirety of their working life. An important element of this was a reciprocal loyalty – employer to employee and the reverse. Today this kind of unwritten contract hardly exists in Western industry. The marriages that are undertaken are overwhelmingly marriages of convenience, almost as though the business world had adopted the cohabitation habits of many modern couples.

In sum, the question today is not '*whether* to change', but rather '*when* to change'. The answer to the latter question is likely to be determined by one of the following factors:

1 the logic of your career development;
2 an unfavourable financial situation in your company;
3 conflict;
4 a merger that results in an overpopulation of executive talent;
5 inherent habitual cycles of change within the individual.

DEPARTURE FOLLOWING THE LOGIC OF CAREER DEVELOPMENT

Three or four changes of company before the age of 35 are not only acceptable but increasingly are being seen as evidence of an adaptable, well-rounded personality. These early changes can be made without great risk, since younger executives fortunately are able to find opportunities through such obvious devices as replying to situations vacant advertisements, as well as through more sophisticated methods like executive search firms.

However, change for the sake of change hardly falls under the rubric of 'the logic of career development'. Each change should make sense in the medium and long range context of your career evolution. Just to change in order to obtain a better salary, for example, may make sense in the short term, while proving to be nothing short of damaging in the longer perspective. A logical change can be defined as one of the following:

1 a move that enhances your position in your speciality – finance, engineering or research, for example;
2 a move that expands your field of competence, for instance, from engineering to technical sales; or
3 a move that provides an opportunity to work in a foreign country that has not been a part of your previous experience.

You are well advised to ask yourself what is the basic, fundamental motivation that lies behind your own desire to change. If the answer is that you want to escape from an unpleasant situation, this is not necessarily an invalidation of your instinct for change. What is important is to keep your cool and to time your change to your own best advantage. If, on the one hand, your existing situation is becoming intolerable and, on the other, a post that seems interesting is offered to you, the temptation to take the first thing that comes along may be difficult to resist. How much better it is to check out the new possibility in the light of the three definitions of 'logical change' set out above. At the same time, there are other questions to be asked. Is the company that is making the offer financially sound? What is the nature of its human relations? What is its style of management?

Even relatively early in one's career, it is of course desirable to avoid making a false move. You can check the financial side of most companies through consulting such credit rating agencies as Dun and Bradstreet, Moody's, or Value Line. As concerns such aspects as management ambience, ask a person who is strategically placed in a competitive enterprise. This is not as difficult as it sounds. You might ask a friend or personal contact to give you an introduction to someone in the same sector of activity as the company you are contemplating joining. Even if the friend does not know of someone directly in the domain in question, they might well be able to suggest a person in a related activity who, in their turn, could lead you to the competitor you seek. The information you receive from competitor is frequently more realistic than anything you might hear directly from a member of the enterprise itself.

Age also presents its own logic in terms of career development. The American psychologist Daniel Levenson discovered this fact in his study of the interior development of the adult male. The two periods of transition he identified and which concern us here are the Early Adult transition and the Mid Life transition. Why are the years 28 to 32 and again 38 to 42 so often marked by important career changes? The reasons are not hard to identify. The first period of transition frequently represents consolidation. The individual has been through a long process of learning from others – from parents and teachers – followed by several years of experience in 'real life', including the world of work. They have coped with starting jobs, and may have acquired a spouse and maybe a child or two. Now, perhaps unconsciously, the person is aware that the time has come to review their situation, to consolidate the adult experience with the learning experience, and to seek out the most rewarding paths to the future. There is a strong urge to change. If this inner message is ignored a person emerging from the period of Early Adult transition can experience disappointment and regret in the later phases of their career.

A similar motivation for assessment and change is a part of the Mid Life transition. However, the ingredients for reflection are different. With the arrival of our fortieth birthday, we more often than not are aware, profoundly if not consciously, that our life span may be half over. As a result, questions abound. Am I really satisfied with the work I am doing? What does the future hold if I continue as I am? Are there other, more fulfilling ways of spending my working hours than at present? If so, what are the realistic elements that might or might not warrant a change? The result of this self-questioning can often be that in the end the person decides to stay where they are, while trying to optimise the situation within their present organisation. Or they might choose to risk a change. Either way, the person has avoided the real danger; this is to fail to pay attention to the feelings of restlessness that can build up to a disagreeable climax in the years to come if they continue to be ignored.

DEPARTURE DUE TO AN UNFAVOURABLE FINANCIAL SITUATION WITHIN YOUR COMPANY

Few career problems are trickier to deal with than resolving the question of how to behave in the face of a deteriorating balance sheet. The easy answer, of course, is to leave a sinking ship. For certain people this is not an acceptable solution unless and until the situation shows itself to be verging on the hopeless. These people are like good sportsplayers. For them to quit in the face of adversity is not as easy as it sounds. This is particularly true if one is a part of a good team and if the leader of the company has inspired the kind of loyalty that, for example, Lee Iacocca was able to generate among the employees and the executive team of Chrysler.

On the other hand, we know that we have a loyalty to ourselves and particularly to our families that cannot be ignored. Thus we are in danger of being torn between two conflicting considerations that have one thing in common; they are both rooted in emotion. If ever there is a time for dispassionate appraisal of a situation this is it. Asking the following questions can help in this process.

1 What is the percentage of loss against revenues? Against capital?
2 Has the loss been widening or narrowing over a three-year period?
3 What are the chances of augmenting the capital through new investments? If one way out is a merger, what are your own chances of survival as a member of the weaker team?
4 How great is your faith in your management? Is it based on mere 'liking', even sympathy, or do you feel, objectively, that the company is in the hands of winners?
5 Linked to question 4 is this question: what is the state of morale among the members of staff? Are they continuing the fight or are they filling the air with defeatist talk?
6 What specific, tangible steps are being taken to redress the situation? Is management hesitating too long in its decision to reduce staff? Are they cutting flesh or are they cutting bone – for example sacrificing research and development, while protecting large front office phalanxes?

The stakes are very simple and very important to define. If you remain in your job, a negative assessment of the above points may very well mean that you could abruptly find yourself out of a job and probably without a satisfactory settlement to tide you over a period of unemployment. On the other hand, if the signs look good for a recovery, you are almost sure to end up as a member of a leaner, stronger team. Not only that, but you will have received high marks for your staunchness when the going was rough. The combination of these positive factors can strengthen your position enormously within your company. The number of turnaround situations that can be cited in so many troubled industries in recent years is sufficient testimony to the fact that it is good advice to look carefully before you leap from a ship that is battling stormy seas.

In this discussion we should not overlook one obvious possibility: in the face of a rapid deterioration of the company's situation, the choice of when and how to depart may well be outside your control.

DEPARTURE DUE TO CONFLICT

Earlier we discussed the manifold sources of misunderstanding, genuine differences and conflict that can exist between human beings within an organisation. However, up to now my emphasis has been for the most part on how to work out – or work through – such differences. None the less, there can come a point where the disagreement between superior and subordinate is clearly unworkable. My purpose now is not to try to examine the rights and wrongs that can be charged to the account of one party or the other. We will simply assume that a break is inevitable and address ourselves to the question of how to escape from the situation with the least possible damage to yourself.

Several choices exist. First, you could ask for a meeting with the superior in question and state your intention to leave the organisation. A second possibility is to conduct a quiet, discreet search for opportunities outside your enterprise. A third choice might be to keep your thoughts to yourself and to await a first move from your boss in the hope of negotiating an important settlement.

In weighing up these possibilities, there is one transcendent factor to keep in mind. How will your departure affect your future career progression? Choice number 1 – informing your boss in advance of your intention to depart – is virtually to ensure that you will be put promptly on the sidelines of all meaningful activity. You also risk the danger of a summons later to the office of your superior who is likely to announce that, because of its lack of content, your post has become 'redundant' and therefore is to be eliminated. In this case, you may find yourself that anathema of executive search people – the unemployed executive.

Choice number 2 is to conduct a 'quiet research' of the job market and then, having signed an employment contract elsewhere, to tip-toe away quietly. This move sounds more plausible than, in reality, it is. A 'quiet' job search is usually a protracted job search – in itself a disadvantage. More inconvenient still, a prolonged period of search can well mean that you might have one proposition one month, another the next and a third the next month. How is it possible to evaluate one offer against another, given such a time lapse? Finally, having made your decision, you will leave your com-pany without a financial settlement; in other words, you have allowed your adversary a complete victory.

The third choice – wait for your boss to make the first move – may bring you short-term gains in the form of some kind of favourable termination settlement. Keep in mind, however, that prospective employers, perhaps preceded by an executive searcher, will demand references from your most recent employer. Since you have set your-self up to be branded 'difficult' by, in effect, inviting a firing, such references are hardly likely to be very favourable.

Happily there is a fourth way of proceeding. This is quietly to make all of your preparations for a job search, and then to mount a swift and well-coordinated attack on the job market.

It does not matter if your boss has some hints of your research. You may even be called into the boss's office to be confronted with the fact that they have wind of what's going on. Keep your cool. Your answer could well be a question, for example, 'What makes you think I am looking around?' If the boss has heard it from someone, you can shrug and reply that from time to time you have contacts with head hunters. On the other hand, if some contact of another company has passed the boss a letter you have written, your reaction might be to say that it is only natural for you to explore the job market periodi-cally in order to verify that your progress is in line with that of others of your age and experience. In other words, under no circumstances is it wise to be dragged into an admission that your intention is to leave the company. If you do, you are then only a step from submit-ting your resignation.

In any case, your adversary will probably be relieved that you are putting into motion the wheels of your departure. Now they at least begin to see the end of their 'problems' with a dissident subordinate and your adversary is likely to be highly cooperative in the matter of requests for references. Who knows, your adversary might even wax enthusiastic in touting you into a job outside your company.

While most such 'leaks' are without real consequence, I can think of a number that have proved to be downright beneficial. Take the case of Harry Y who found himself buried under an incompetent and jealous boss, the head of the London subsidiary of the large electronics company that was Harry's employer. A request for a reference coming from an executive search firm somehow found its way to the chairperson of the company in New York. It so happened that the chairperson and Harry had, some years earlier, worked together on a start-up operation in California. In the course of their collaboration, Harry won the chairperson's respect and liking. Learning that Harry intended to leave the company, the chief was furious, but not towards Harry. His spleen was directed towards the London manager who had failed to profit from Harry's very real abilities. Harry was summoned to New York and handed an assignment to conduct a market study of the company's potential in the Middle East. He made a brilliant analysis of the situation there – so brilliant that he was asked to give his presentation to the various units of the corporation scattered about the USA. The solution to Harry's problem came swiftly. He was assigned to Saudi Arabia as marketing manager charged with the development of the company's operations there.

DEPARTURE BECAUSE OF A MERGER

When word reaches you of an impending merger of your company with another, one question is all important: which is to be the dominant partner? If the answer is 'the other side', you may well assume that there will be overcrowding at most management levels and that the first people to be singled out for redundancy will be those within your own company.

There are exceptions, of course. The dominant partner may well need the know-how and experience of some executives from the other side. Beware, however, of the siren call that attempts to make you feel wanted, even to a degree indispensable. We have already cited one instance of a general manager who heeded this call, only to find himself 'extruded' once he had smoothed the way through the transitional period following a merger. The only safe course of action in this case is to mount an active job search. Once you have found a solid possibility elsewhere, you can confront your management with an offer to negotiate your departure. Look the other person steadily in the eye during this conversation. You should be able to divine their intentions towards you – whether there is relief at the prospect of your departure, whether they want to seduce you into staying for practical reasons of transition or whether you are seen as a permanent member of the new, fused organisation. Evidence of this last attitude takes the form of an increase in your salary. Money, as they say, speaks louder (in this case) than words.

DEPARTURE DUE TO YOUR OWN INNER CYCLES

Not surprisingly, many people overlook the fact that changes in their life occur with a certain stated frequency. None the less this is an important piece of information for us to have if we are to control the evolution of our career, rather than being influenced by what may seem to be a series of accidents. Some psychologists say that there are no accidents in the life of a human being. I cannot go so far as that. However, I do know, with certainty, that things happen to us that appear to be the result of chance but on examination have, after all, a logical explanation. Not infrequently the hidden reason has to do with cycles, those mysterious periodic changes that seem to occur with a certain regularity – unless consciously interrupted – throughout a person's life span.

Typical cycle number 1

Your father is a diplomat, an engineer, a military or naval man. The early conditioning of children of fathers in these occupations often includes regular changes of home, of region and perhaps of country. The message repeatedly received in the impressionable years of such a youngster is clear. No situation is likely to last. Not only that, changes in certain professions are made with regularity. Every two or three years is typical. Soon a rhythm is set up inside the developing personality. It says, somewhere in the subconscious: 'Three years? Time to move on.' Thus the cycle is established. Throughout your early adult years – and perhaps far beyond that – the same insistent voice keeps chiming at the same intervals, now there must be a change.

The danger here is evident. Any impulse to change must be carefully examined as to the real merits of a specific new activity to be certain that the move contemplated is really a positive, rather than a subjectively motivated, choice for the future.

Typical cycle number 2

Many educational systems carry the seeds of a two-to-four-year cycle. In England and Wales, for instance this means two years of GCSEs, two years of A levels, followed by three or perhaps four years of university. People who have been 'programmed' by their parents to excel at each step of the educational process come to see life in terms of such relatively short-term objectives. Beyond the next exam, the programme goes, nothing else counts. It is not too surprising that many people who have been presented with this series of short-term goals end up in some sort of project management. Typical of such jobs are those that involve specific construction or engineering projects, or perhaps consultancy assignments that form a string of relatively short-term challenges. There is a certain merit in this (probably unconscious) choice of career, but the merit diminishes with the onset of the second half of your working life. Thereafter, the absence of a clear, long-term goal may become psychologically troublesome. At this point the mid life change frequently takes a hand in the form of a hunger for more permanency and – as a result – the commencement of a job search that is oriented toward this end.

Typical cycle number 3

Apparently not imposed by early conditioning, as in the case of the two cycles discussed above, the seven-year cycle seems to have its origins in folklore and cultural history. Most people have heard of 'the seven-year itch', the 'seven fat and the seven lean years' and the seven-year periods of indenture that chained the frustrated Jacob to the wily Laban. Some lives are profoundly affected by a kind of unconscious slavery to a seven-year cycle. The fact that this particular cycle defies analysis, in contrast to the others, makes it even more difficult to detect and therefore to deal with.

What you can do is trace back the events of your own life. If you find that important changes have occurred regularly at approximately seven-year intervals, you are well advised to project ahead in order to anticipate the next likely date of change. There is nothing predestined or inevitable about either this or the other two cycles. Because the changes are unconsciously motivated, they can be neutralised by paying conscious attention to the likelihood of their repetition. In this way it becomes possible to substitute rational decision making for an irrational process that, until now, may have gone unrecognised.

HOW TO SAY GOODBYE

Two radically different circumstances of departure from an enterprise are easy to identify. They can be summed up as either 'voluntary' or 'involuntary' situations. Let us dispose of the latter first, since it at least has the dubious merit of being relatively uncomplicated.

I am going to assume that you have correctly protected your own interests by arriving at the best possible financial settlement, as provided for by your contract. As a part of these negotiations you may also want to check your company's policy on 'outplacement' and to find out if this kind of aid is available to you. (Outplacement is a service, paid for by your company, to provide professional help to departing employees in the matter of seeking and finding a satisfactory new post.)

Another question that frequently arises is the manner in which your terminal pay is paid out to you. Should you accept a lump-sum cheque, or is it better to continue to receive your salary on a regular basis until the total amount due has been distributed to you? Putting aside the matter of which method is preferable in terms of your income tax liability, I strongly favour a periodical pay-out in the form of a continued salary. By opting for this method, you will be able to say that you are still an employee of your company rather than someone 'between jobs'. Naturally your employer will have a say in the procedure selected. However, if they are truly cooperative, they may not only agree to continue your regular salary payments, but help you in other ways – the use of an office, for example, or arrangements with the switchboard to handle your calls in a discreet fashion.

Even under the best of circumstances, handling the psychological fall-out from being 'let go' is likely to be anything but easy. Whether a firing is due to a 'reorganisation' or to some short-fall in the individual's performance, the event may well produce some bitterness. (Even if the decision was made for 'financial reasons', the victim may be moved to ask 'Why me and not him?') No matter what the degree of your disappointment or sense of injustice is, a word to the wise says that you are well advised not to indulge in a display of feelings. You may be particularly tempted to sound off in the presence of sympathetic colleagues and subordinates. Before doing so, remember that their sympathy costs them nothing, whereas protecting their jobs is to them a matter of vital, practical importance. Not only is it going to be fruitless to air your resentment, but word of your comments may readily leak – or be leaked – back to your employer. The attitude you show while in the process of leaving can well colour the kind of references you will get – even their tone of voice on the telephone with a future employer asking their opinion of you. I am not against the idea of your conducting a firm negotiation with your company. I am simply saying you should check your emotions during those last days on the job.

The voluntary departure

Apart from questions of health, there is likely to be only one sound reason for making a voluntary exit from your organisation. This is because you have found a new and better post elsewhere. I know that there are days, weeks and months in everyone's working life where the desire to escape seems overwhelming. If, however, you have family responsibilities, think twice. We have mentioned the prejudice that exists among professional recruiters against recommending unemployed executives for jobs. I use the word 'prejudice' in its literal meaning of 'pre-judged'. We all know that there are many valuable people who are in search of employment. Most of them are out of a job for no blameworthy reason at all. They may even have demonstrated their courage in voluntarily putting to an end an unsatisfactory situation. Yet the fact that they are 'out' works against them. Better by far to remain 'in', regardless of the discomfort that may be involved.

My assumption here is that you have, indeed, stuck by your post while conducting a successful search for a new position. Not uncommonly, a feeling of euphoria and relief accompanies the handshake closing a deal, and signalling the end of a period of uncertainty and exposure to the slings and arrows of outrageous recruiters.

The question of timing

How much notice must you give your company before leaving? If the subject is not covered by contract, this is a matter to be negotiated. However, let us suppose that your new employer is pressing you for an early arrival because of an important vacancy in their organisation. You are liable to be torn, in this case, between doing 'the right thing' for your present company and wanting to meet the needs of your future management. The problem, in reality, is not as stark as it seems. Few employers want to shackle in place a person who clearly would prefer to be gone. After all, a person who remains in a company under duress is hardly likely to be the most motivated (or motivating) of executives. Intelligent management will, of course, insist that the person's workload be disposed of in an orderly fashion, but beyond that it will recognise the negative effect a demotivated person can have on colleagues and subordinates.

Let us suppose, on the other hand, that your management is not inclined to be so reasonable. This is particularly likely to be the case if you are leaving to join a competitor. Here is a situation that requires all the objectivity you can muster. Naturally you will not want to leave behind any more bitterness than is intrinsic to the situation. On the other hand your future is with your new employer. If you have been hired to fill a critical vacancy and your future company will suffer from an exaggerated delay, you might be justified in leaving sooner than your employer demands. You will have to explain the facts to the employer, to affirm that you are not leaving behind any unfinished business and then to negotiate firmly the earliest possible date of departure. While this may not be easy to put into action, keep one thought in mind. No one is indispensable. Companies survive changes of personnel whether or not the changes meet with their convenience. On the other hand, the individual's career – yours – is protected neither, probably, by large amounts of capital nor by the trappings of power. So, you must act in your own best interests, using whatever leverage is at your command. In short, your career evolution during the years to come is at stake, whereas the company will soon remember your departure, if it remembers it at all, as a minor inconvenience.

A better offer comes along

A well-organised and active search of the job market may well turn up multiple possibilities for the future. It is not unusual for a person to accept one attractive offer, only to have another, even better, one materialise shortly thereafter. This can pose a dilemma that is not easy to solve. Joseph W, a journalist, found himself in just such a situation. He was delighted to be asked to become features editor of a magazine – covering restaurants, shopping, theatre, books and so on. The post promised good pay, a certain prestige and a lot of variety.

However, as a result of his earlier contacts, Joe was quite unexpectedly offered the position of managing director of an important news service, worldwide in its scope. The second job was clearly the more attractive of the two but Joe was troubled by the fact that he had signed a contract with the magazine. None the less, after talks with his wife and a long inner debate, he decided to confront the managing editor of the magazine with the news that he would not be honouring his contract. Mentally prepared for a disagreeable meeting, Joe was astounded by the reaction of the editor. Instead of berating Joe, he said that he understood – that a person should go where his heart and best judgement dictated. Further, he said, he would be the last person to want to have on his staff someone who would rather be elsewhere. 'Do you really think', he asked, 'that such a person would be giving the best of himself in a job he considered to be second best?' To Joe's stupefaction the man congratulated him on his new post and suggested they keep in touch. He even proposed that they lunch together.

Such conflicts are not always resolved so happily, but the principle is one to keep in mind. You are doing no one – yourself or a company – a service by clinging to the letter of a contract, rather than following the dictates of your own true feelings.

STARTING ANEW

Even the most constructive job change carries with it the risk that inevitably accompanies a move into the unknown. In spite of your diligent research into the facts about your future employer – financial situation, style of management, human relations ambience – you can never have the feeling of your new environment until you are a part of it. As a result, the facts and impressions you pick up during your first weeks in the new job will have much to do with the enthusiasm, or lack of it, with which you launch into the future. However, the reverse is also true. The patterns of relationships and the way others perceive you may be indelibly fixed within three months or less of your arrival. For this reason I always recommend that my clients observe the following cardinal principles when starting out in a new organisation.

Keep a low profile

Do not give in to the urge to display your brilliance and creativity, thereby hoping to win the attention and approval of your hierarchy. You may, instead, arouse the competitive hormones of your colleagues before you have acquired sufficient concrete knowledge and experience to deal effectively with their rivalry. In the role of a newcomer, a little humility can go a long way towards speeding your integration into the group.

Listen

Few people really listen. Many, on the other hand, are skilled at appearing to listen while their mind is elsewhere. The American psychoanalyst Theodore Reik spoke of 'listening with the third ear'. He meant that it is not enough to hear just the words, but also to catch the cadence and the tone of voice of the person you are speaking with in order to perceive the real message they are conveying. If ever there was a time to bring into play this talent, the start of a new position is among the most important. Because it is not necessary – and it is even contraindicated – to 'sell yourself' during these early days, you are in an ideal position to ask questions and to observe.

Make no pals

Earlier I spoke of a newly-arrived executive who was nearly seduced into an office war by an overly-friendly colleague intent on setting up his own personal circle of influence within the company. While I dislike seeming to recommend suspicion as an element in your approach to your new colleagues, I do suggest that you reflect first, rather than entering too quickly into friendships and alliances. Those can come later, perhaps, after you have had a real opportunity to get to know the qualities of the cast of characters with whom you are now involved.

Don't spurn small talk

Many intelligent people feel that verbal communication in business is designed solely to convey pragmatic messages of a certain substance and importance. In other words, they rule out chats about the weather, or sports, or the events of the day on the ground that time so spent is unproductive. Lofty as this attitude is, it overlooks the fact that human beings share some of the characteristics to be found in nature on a more basic level. When animals sniff and circle each other on meeting they are evincing a desire to assess the nature and intentions of the new contact before entering into a more direct relationship. I feel that a certain amount of 'small talk' serves the same purpose. Apart from its value in establishing human contact, small talk is a non-threatening way of reaching some understanding of the character of the other person before entering, perhaps, into a more meaningful relationship.

Keep it simple

To reflect your commitment to your new organisation, you might well bring a few personal touches into your office – books, knick-knacks, pictures – depending on your observation of the practices within the company. This is a good way to signal that you have come to stay. However, you will want to draw the line at 'showy' items such as expensive paintings, silver picture frames or massive pen-and-pencil sets. Above all, be restrained in the requests you make for office furniture and fixtures. The little luxuries can come later. For the moment, your display of a low profile is linked to your physical surroundings, as well as to your modest initial display of our talents.

We have now come full circle in our discussion of the use of 'political' techniques in the advancement of your career. Having passed through the first testing period, you are now in a position to bring into play the principles set out in the preceding chapters. In the next chapter you will find a summary of the main points of the book.

CHAPTER 20

In conclusion

Everyone is aware that the world of business is becoming internationalised at a rapidly increasing pace. It is hardly surprising then that individual flexibility and adaptability are qualities that are deemed to be indispensable. Almost every day we read of astonishing corporate marriages. A Japanese consortium takes over a Californian property company. A French firm acquires an American cosmetic company. An American group swallows up a British pharmaceutical producer. Adding to this list of international marriages and takeovers is an easy exercise for anyone who reads the business press.

So far we have laid down certain general principles of kinetic human relations. Good sense alone dictates that international buyouts, mergers and partnerships may well modify any generalised, universal model we may try to create of proactive executive behaviour. For example the separation between professional and personal lives is far more marked in a French than in an American context. The use of first names comes much more easily to British colleagues than to Germans working together. The idea of multiple changes of company on the part of an executive may be acceptable – and even seen as a plus – in Europe and America, but is frowned upon by the Japanese. And so the list of variables and mutations grows.

Such evident differences notwithstanding, I am repeatedly struck, not by the differences between nationalities but by the basic communality of feelings I find among my clients of differing origins. Strip away the layers of fashion, of cultural encrustation, even of religion and you arrive at certain basic predictable human responses to a variety of stimuli. Thus it becomes possible to produce a Hollywood thriller that will generate a similar audience reaction around the world or an opera that moves the emotions of the inhabitants of the seven continents, as indeed do the Olympic games and the works of the Impressionist painters.

However, it is, of course, not only national influences that shape a specific corporate culture. One of the most marked differences in mentality is that existing between executives in small and in large companies. In the latter context, the individual functions in a field of action are clearly delimited by a detailed and often complex organisation chart. Within a smaller company the luxury of hiring specialists to handle long-range planning, treasury matters, in-depth market research or general services is often non-existent. By necessity you become a Jack or Jill of many trades, with the result that you may have direct contact with the people who activate all of the levers of the enterprise. (Lucky is the younger person who is in a well-managed subsidiary within a well-managed large group of companies. Such a person has the possibility of benefitting from a variety of job challenges, while at the same time being exposed to modern management techniques at a level of sophistication found only in larger – and richer – organisations.)

An even greater difference in corporate personality is to be found between the nimble, fast-moving world of high-tech and the vast, often cumbersome enterprises in what can be loosely described as the public sector. These include some of the great private utility companies as well as enterprises, such as those in public transport, that are partly or wholly government owned. The contrast between British Air and British Rail makes the point. In the first category creativity and intuition, as well as sound professional discipline, are highly prized. In the latter, executive progress is linked more often than not to the number of years of service performed and the ability to stay out of trouble – to make no waves.

Obviously there are many other, less clearly opposed styles of management. Some companies – particularly banks and law firms – recruit chiefly from the 'best schools and universities'. This sets up an undertone of unvoiced snobbery which sometimes verges on the creation of a mafia and which can pose a very special problem for the uninitiated. The difference is vast between such an atmosphere, and that of a company founded and managed by a person who won out solely by virtue of intelligence and energy.

While keeping in mind all such possible differences, I am listing below 'ten commandments' that seem to me to apply universally. They are intended to identify and to distill those elements of pro-activity that are likely to be useful in all – or nearly all – corporate situations.

COMMANDMENT 1: KNOW THYSELF

What are your goals? Are they borrowed or are they real? Borrowed goals are those imposed upon us by others – perhaps by our parents, perhaps by well-meaning instructors or even by the social context in which we are brought up. A proposed career course coming from an uncle at a peak of a young person's opposition to his father may sway the decision away from the father's wishes, but for spurious reasons. An ambitious mother not infrequently will set forth unrealistically high career expectations for her idolised child. An antipathy for sales and marketing in a family of a certain social status may deflect a young person from a career for which they are ideally suited. However, the most frequent source of ill-fitting jobs is discussed in Chapter 1 where guidance is given in sorting out an individual's mix of line and staff characteristics. The person who is driven to show concrete results of their activities will be miserable in, for example, a marketing analysis post. Conversely, there are too many unfortunate cases of serious and reflective people being thrust – because of their good work in a staff role – into responsibilities for which they have neither the taste nor the talent.

COMMANDMENT 2: LOOK UPWARDS

How easy it is to become totally involved in the challenge at hand – to concern ourselves with the performance of others and with the results stemming from the specific project under way. This kind of dedication is not easy to criticise. However, it can be dangerous in the sense that we risk losing contact with the source of nourishment for the enterprise and for ourselves as individual members of the enterprise. I refer, of course, to the hierarchy of power above us. Unless you have your own business, fully capitalized by yourself, you are bound to be responsible to some person or group of people (eg your shareholders). It is unsafe to assume that your superior is, through some sort of telepathy, aware of your activities, your problems and/or your progress. It may even be insulting to assume that a lack of interest on your boss's part in the operations for which they are responsible would make contact with the boss extraneous and without purpose. Keep in touch. It is better to risk making a nuisance of yourself through too much upward communication than to risk getting out of touch with your boss's thinking – not only with their opinion of your performance but also with their evolving views on your company's structure, direction and management. Ask for meetings. Send written reports if all else fails. But never, never overlook the importance of keeping in regular contact.

COMMANDMENT 3: KNOW WHEN TO SAY NO

Overload is one of the most dangerous positions in which you can find yourself as an executive. You may be deep in the critical stages of a project when you are told to fly to such and such a city to deal with a certain situation. Or you are asked to add an extra region to your sales responsibilities but without added help. Many people in such situations fear that a refusal to accept the added burden will be a black mark in their record. Indeed this may temporarily be the case, but much depends on how your refusal is made. A well-documented, unemotional presentation of the current use of your time, showing clearly the danger to the company's interests of adding activities to your current workload, may well drive home the point. And the danger is very real. A manager who is spread too thin may risk losing control not only of new and added assignments, but of their main responsibility as well. This is the road to burn-out, a culmination that is useful neither to the individual nor to the enterprise.

COMMANDMENT 4: DECOMPARTMENTALISE

If your organisation is a part of the Western industrialised world, you may already be aware of the amount of business that is transacted outside the office – in clubs, restaurants and homes. (Even, in one the less appetizing American innovations, at breakfast!) If you are not so aware, this is a clear reversal of the adage, 'What you don't know won't hurt you'. No longer is it possible to arrange your professional life in compartments: the office here and all the rest elsewhere. The mingling of business and pleasure is found in many forms. It takes place at business conventions and professional meetings. It happens when you and your spouse receive visitors from another country. Christmas and farewell parties, receptions, invitations to one another's homes are all combining to break down the barriers between office and private life. The person who attempts to stay aloof from such extra-business contact is – probably without being aware of it – damaging their career. Since wives and husbands are often a part of evening activities, the spouse must clearly understand the equation:

when required, either join in with good grace, or accept the proba-bility of an ultimately restricted level of status and income for the family.

COMMANDMENT 5: PLAY IT STRAIGHT

No line in this book should be construed as recommending trickiness or deception among the possible tools of progression. A person's reputation for integrity is gained slowly, month by month, year by year. It can be lost in a day. I hope I have made abundantly clear in these pages the difference between proactivity and charlatanism. The charlatan speaks untruths; the proactive person understands that it is not always necessary or useful to say everything that is on their mind. The charlatan will praise a poor boss; the proactive individual will not try to hide approval of a good boss. The charlatan will be ingratiating to a person's face, but will talk negatively about them behind their back; the proactive person will either speak their mind directly to the other, if useful, or will hold their peace. Finally, the charlatan will put their own good before the good of the company; the proactive person understands the real meaning of 'charity begins at home'.

COMMANDMENT 6: BE SAFE, NOT SORRY

Several of the problems described in the case studies in this book have one basic cause: indiscretion. Confidential papers not suf-ficiently protected, too much confidence placed in unworthy persons, failure to 'get it in writing' – all of these have resulted in serious career setbacks for the people involved. Largely responsible for such lapses is the well-defined psychological phenomenon called 'projec-tion'. We all have a tendency to ascribe to others our own motiva-tions. Decent, trustworthy people find it difficult to believe that a person would go through someone's private papers for 'useful' confidential material. The idea of another person's breaking a shared confidence is equally outside of the scope of their imaginings. So, too, is the thought that a verbal agreement might not in the end be honoured. This may be the moment to suggest, if a bit ruefully, that good people have a certain inbuilt vulnerability in the matter of insufficient caution. The only antidote is for such trusting people to stop and think for just one critical moment: 'What could be the consequences if I fail to stop and think at this moment which, potentially at least, could be critical?'

COMMANDMENT 7: BEWARE OF HUBRIS

Few human sentiments are more dangerous than the sentiment of hubris, the feeling of omnipotence that comes to some executives on the heels of a success or a series of successes. Quite probably the flight of Icarus was fuelled by his conviction that only 'the sky was his limit'. It is a fair guess that the wax that melted from his wings in the glare of the sun probably did so gradually. In executive careers the fall is sometimes more precipitous. My experience in working with clients demonstrates that success can be almost as dangerous as failure. You feel a deep conviction that in some way the gods – or the zodiac or karma – are on your side. You are blinded to the possibility of stepping on a banana skin whether it happens to be there by accident or placed by some person's design. Only one sure protection exists against such situations and it can be summed up by the word humility. It is fine to demonstrate to the world of employees, bosses and clients all the charisma you can muster; but never forget that, somewhere inside of all of us, there still lives a child who has need of the love and support of others. And what is equally important is that those others have the same need which you can only ignore at your own peril. The danger of hubris – the blind love of oneself – is that it can blind us to both needs.

COMMANDMENT 8: BEWARE ALSO OF MEMOS

From time to time nearly everyone feels the need to let off steam. The logical way, indeed the safe way, often seems to do so by means of a well-constructed memorandum, sometimes copied to interested parties. Obviously written communications are a part of normal office procedure. However, the particular kind of memos I am speaking of have an underlying emotional content. They plead a cause, or defend a position, or try to straighten out a misunderstanding. I maintain that this type of message is nearly always more productively delivered in person. The difficulty lies in the impossibility of predicting the mood of the recipient. If the recipient is hard pressed with other problems, business or domestic, they might react with hostility even to a message that the writer deems to be a model of objectivity. Since the signer is not present at the time the words are received they have no way to gauge the reaction of the target and to respond to it appropriately. Conversely, in a face-to-face discussion, the reactions are very likely to be clear and thus can be dealt with on the spot, thereby avoiding a build-up of pressure.

Is there a good test for choosing between a written and verbal approach? Yes. Ask yourself exactly why you are thinking of writing. Do you fear a rejection or a confrontation? This may mean that in reality you are choosing an indirect form of communication in order to evade, rather than to deal with, the situation. If so, the signal is clear: arrange an appointment for a meeting.

COMMANDMENT 9: USE HUMOUR, BUT SPARINGLY

Americans seem to appreciate the value of humour in business more than most other nationalities. They correctly see it as a way to release tension, to disarm the opposition and even to discharge aggression. However, it is important not to exaggerate. A person with a good sense of humour may find an appreciative audience for their little jokes. As a result they can be tempted too often to exercise their talents, with the result that they are no longer regarded by others as a 'serious' person. Even more dangerous is humour that may verge on sarcasm. Others will sense, probably correctly, that behind the levity there is a suppressed aggression. In this case whatever humour might exist curdles into discomfort and, perhaps, ill-feeling. Yes, humour is prescribed at the right moments, but always in moderation.

COMMANDMENT 10: DECIDED TO LEAVE? DON'T DAWDLE

There are many reasons that people find the path upwards inside their company to be blocked: poor financial results may have halted expansion; the company is on the junior side of a merger, with people from the dominant partner filling the best posts; all the important positions are filled by young people; a serious difference exists with your immediate superior. Whatever the reason, you must make a clear decision. You may elect to stay in the organisation in the vague hope that things might improve – or you may decide to search else-where. My plea here is not that you chose one course of action or the other. It is that you act promptly if you decide to move. The situation is not unlike that created between husband and wife when one or the other has made up their mind to divorce. The mental atmosphere deteriorates on both sides to the point of unpleasant consequences such as, in a professional context, a decision on the part of your employer to take the initiative in a separation. Far more proactive is to conduct a crisp, intensive search outside, to choose your future post and then to negotiate the most satisfactory terms for your departure that you can. Then, problem solved, you might arrange a holiday to clear your mind in preparation for your new role. If you leave with a smile, the chances are that you will enter with a smile into your new situation. In short, you will be off to a good start.